JN092813

英 語 で 伝 え る

茶の湯の銘
100

100
BEAUTIFUL WORDS
IN THE WAY OF TEA

ブルース・濱名宗整

Bruce Hamana Sosei

淡交社

水温む | *Mizunurumu*

寒さが緩み、氷と雪がとけ、沼や池の水があたたまってきたように見えること。水底で眠っていた魚は動きはじめ、水辺の植物が育ちはじめる。自然の事象のなかに春が感じられる。

Mizunurumu means water warming in spring. The cold becomes less intense; the ice and snow melt; and water in the marshes and lakes becomes warmer. Fish that had been dormant in the riverbeds and lake bottoms begin to move about, and the plants in and around the water begin to grow. Spring can be felt in the movement of things in nature.

春の泊 | *Haru no tomari*

刻々と過ぎゆく春のこと。あらゆるものに生命の喜びが溢れ、過ごしやすく楽しい季節、そんな春の終わりを表わす言葉は多くある。こうした言葉は時間の流れを捉え、過ぎ行く春を惜しむ感情を強く表す。関連する語に、「春の湊」、「春の果」、「春の別れ」、「春のかたみ」、「行く春」がある。

Haru no tomari means spring which departs moment by moment. Many words express the egress of spring, the season when things are filled with the joy of life, and the weather is comfortable and pleasant. This phrase captures the flow of time and emphasizes the sense of lamenting the passing of spring. Related terms are *haru no minato* "arrival at the end of spring," *haru no hate* "the limit of spring," *haru no wakare* "spring's departure," *haru no katami* "remembrance of spring," and *yuku haru* "passing spring."

夏
SUMMER

星祭 | *Hoshi matsuri*

旧暦の7月7日、現在のグレゴリオ暦で7月7日もしくは8月7日に行われる七夕のこと。現在の七夕は中国と日本の行事が組み合わさったもので、両方の要素が合体している。中国では、牽牛星と織女星が出会うとされる日に、七夕と呼ばれる行事が行われる。日本の行事は、棚機つ女の伝説に基づいているが、この棚機つ女は水辺の小屋で身を清め、先祖の魂を迎えるために布を織ったといわれている。江戸時代には伝統芸能や学問の上達を祈る風習となった。里芋の葉の上の夜露を集めて墨を磨り、5色の短冊に願いを書いた。この短冊は笹竹に結んで飾られた。関連語に「七夕」「星迎え」「星合」がある。

Hoshi matsuri means the star festival which is observed on the seventh day of the seventh lunar month, now July 7th or August 7th of the Gregorian calendar. The present star festival is a combination of Chinese and Japanese observances and a synthesis of elements from both. In China, the observance of *Shichiseki* is thought to be the one day of the year when the Oxherd (*Kengyusei*, the star Altair) and the Weaving Princess (*Shokujosei*, the star Vega) are able to meet. In Japan, the observance is based on the legend of *Tanabatatsume* "the weaving maiden," who purified herself in a hut at the waterside in order to weave cloth to welcome the spirits of the ancestors. In the Edo Period, the observance became a ritual prayer for advancement in the traditional performing arts and scholarship. Dew that formed on taro leaves at night was gathered and used to make ink which was then used to write wishes on five-colored strips of paper. These colored strips were offered by being tied to bamboo branches. Related terms are *Tanabata* "Seventh Night," *hoshimukae* "greeting the stars," and *hoshiai* "star meeting."

若葉雨 | *Wakaba-ame*

新しく鮮やかな葉の上に落ちる初夏の雨のこと。明るい新緑の「若葉」に比べると、「青葉」は夏に豊かに成長する深い緑をさす。この時期に降る雨を「青葉雨」と呼ぶ。

Wakaba-ame is young leaf rain and refers to the early summer rain which falls upon the fresh, verdant leaves. *Wakaba* is a bright, new green, but *aoba* is the deep green of the luxuriant growth of the summer. The rain that falls at that time is called *aoba-ame*.

山路 | *Yamaji*

山中の道のこと。秋には、紅葉や木々の実り、鳥や風のざわめき
が山路を取り囲む。「深山路」は深い山奥の道のことで、世俗を
離れた静けさを感じさせる語。

Yamaji means mountain path. In the autumn, the colors
of the deciduous trees, the bountifulness of fruits and
nuts, the stirrings of the birds and the wind seem to
surround and enclose a path, which winds through the
mountains. *Miyamaji* refers to a road or path deep in the
mountains. The word carries a feelings of seclusion and
peacefulness.

庵の月 | *Iori no tsuki*

人里離れた質素な住居から見る月のこと。静かな雰囲気がひと
きわ深く心に沁み入る。

Irori no tsuki means the moon seen from a rustic abode
far away from human habitation. The quiet atmosphere
permeates ever more deeply into the heart.

WINTER

寒雀 | *Kansuzume*

冬の寒さが厳しい時期、食料が乏しくなり、食べるものを求めて人里に集まる雀がよく見られる。寒さから身を守るため羽が厚くなり、ふっくら丸い見た目になる。関連語に「凍雀」、「ふくら雀」などがある。

Kansuzume means cold sparrow. During the intensely cold part of winter, food becomes scarce and sparrows are often seen gathering near human habitation in search of food. The feathers of the birds become thicker to protect them from the cold, giving them a plump, round appearance. Related terms are *kogoesuzume* "chilled sparrow" and *fukurasuzume* "plump sparrow."

初霞 | *Hatsu-gasumi*

新春に野や山にたなびく霞のこと。

Hatsu-gasumi means the first mist which forms in the
fields and mountains at the New Year.

銘 か ら 学 ぶ

中国や日本では、建物や部屋、船舶、また岩や硯、楽器、刀剣など、気に入っているものや大事にしているものに名前をつけるという習慣が高度に発達してきました。ものにつけるこの名前のことを銘と呼びます。この習慣は茶の湯の世界でも 500 年以上前に取り入れられ、現在まで続いています。美術館では銘で呼ばれる歴史的で有名な茶道具を鑑賞することができます。中でも特に名高い道具は「名物」と呼ばれ、その多くに道具の所有者や作者、称賛者によって銘がつけられています。

ものに名前がつけられているということから、所有者が香合や茶入、茶碗、茶器、茶杓といったものに対して、敬愛の念を持っていたということが分かります。そうした道具を眺め、茶会で使うことを楽しんでいたのです。また、名前をつけることで、ものにある種の力を与える、もしくは名前そのものが命を吹き込む力をもつ、という思想もありました。

銘を学ぶことで、日本人の美意識ばかりか、文学、詩歌、習慣、歴史、また芸能が千利休（1591 年没）の時代以来の「茶人」たちに与えていた影響をも感じとることができます。美しい言葉や名前によって、こうした美術や工芸品の鑑賞に深みと意義が加わり、また銘を理解することが茶人と茶道具との関係を再認識する助けにもなるのです。

「茶事」と呼ばれる、省略なしの正式な茶会のための道具の取り合わせをみれば、季節や自然との調和に対する亭主の気遣いがうかがえます。亭主は道具組の中心となるコンセプトやアイデアを決め、使用する道具の銘をどのように関連づけ、作用させるか考えをめぐらせます。ほとんどの場合、掛物の書を第一に選び、それから他の道具を選びます。茶道具につけられた多くの銘は季節に応じたものですが、季節に関わらず一年を通して使える銘もあります。

Learning from *Gomei*
"Poetic Names"

In China and Japan, the custom of giving names to buildings and their rooms, to boats and ships, and to important or favorite objects, such as rocks, ink stones, musical instruments, and swords, etc., became highly developed. The names given to objects are referred to as *gomei*, "poetic names." In the world of chanoyu, the custom of naming objects was incorporated over 500 years ago and continues to this day. In museums, it is possible to see famed, historic tea utensils recognized by their *gomei*. The most important of these are called *meibutsu* "objects of renown" and many of them feature *gomei* given to them by their owners, creators, or admirers.

Giving names to objects indicates the love and respect that the owner had for objects such as incense containers, flower containers, tea bowls, thick tea containers, and tea scoops, which the owner enjoyed looking at and using in tea gatherings. There was also the belief that conferring a name to an object gave it certain power, or that the name itself contained a spirit which animated the object.

By studying *gomei*, we can gain a glimpse, not only of Japanese aesthetic sensibilities, but also learn about the influence that literature, poetry, customs, history, and the performing arts had on the *chajin* "tea masters" from the time of Sen Rikyu (died, 1591). The beauty of these words and names adds depth and meaning to the appreciation of these art/craft objects. Further, understanding *gomei* helps us recreate the connection that these tea masters had to their tea utensils.

In the selection of utensils for a formal full-length tea gathering called *chaji* "tea gathering or function," we can see the host's concern for harmony with the seasons and the natural world. The host selects a central concept or idea to unite all of the objects and thinks of how the *gomei* of his objects expand and develop the concept. Very often the calligraphy on the hanging scroll is taken as the starting point, and then other objects are selected. Tea utensils may have a *gomei* that has a seasonal reference, but there are others which have *gomei* that are not linked to a certain time of the year and may be used at any time.

銘はデザインのモチーフにもなります。例えば、「山里」というような銘は茶碗や茶入、茶杓につけられることがありますが、のちに棚の名前につけられたり、デザインとして茶碗に描かれたり、文様として棗に描かれることもあります。銘は数百年前から使われているので、茶人や画家、職人はそこから着想を得て、別の媒体で様々な技法を使い、元の銘のコンセプトをさまざまなものに変化させてきました。

茶菓子にも菓銘がつけられますが、多くが季語からとられています。季語は俳句などの和歌で、季節を示すために詠みこむように定められた語のことです。茶の湯の銘は季語も含みますが、季語でない銘もあります。

道具に銘をつける習慣の幅広さと奥深さがわかる『茶の湯の銘大百科』（淡交社、2005 年）は、500 年以上のお茶の歴史から抜粋された約 7,000 語の銘の解説と、様々な茶道具につけられた実際の銘を掲載しています。現在まで、各茶の湯の流派の家元達は、茶事や茶会に使う代表的な茶道具に銘をつけています。

銘は、気象や天文学、動植物、習慣、行事、宗教上の儀式と日本人の生活が深く関わっていることを示す、貴重な情報源です。銘にあらわされた季節感を楽しむことや、銘がつけられた文脈や背景を理解することは、現代の茶の湯において大きな魅力のひとつです。

An original *gomei* may also inspire other design motifs. For example, a poetic name like *Yamazato* "mountain village" may be first given to a tea bowl, thick tea container, or tea scoop. Later it may become used as the name of a *tana* "portable tea stand," the design painted on a tea bowl, or a motif on a lacquered thin tea container. Since *gomei* have been used for several hundred years, tea masters, artists, and craftsmen have found inspiration from them and created many variations of the original concept using different techniques in different media.

Chagashi "confection for chanoyu" very often have been given *kamei*, or "confection names," many of which are *kigo* "seasonal words or phrases," which are included in the writing of haiku and poetry to indicate the season. *Gomei* used in chanoyu may be *kigo*, but there are also *gomei* that are not.

Indicating the breadth and depth of the custom of naming objects, *The Chanoyu no Mei Daihyakka* (The Encyclopedia of Names in Chanoyu, *Tankosha* Publishing, 2005) features about 7,000 *gomei* with explanations and examples of utensils with those *gomei* selected from over 500 years of tea history. Even today, the *iemoto* "grand tea masters" of the various traditions of chanoyu give names to exemplary tea utensils to be used at *chaji* and *chakai* "abbreviated tea gatherings."

Gomei convey information and valuable insight into the close connection between the weather, astronomy, flora and fauna, customs, rituals, religious observances, and the lifestyle of the Japanese people. The enjoyment of the seasonal aspects expressed in the *gomei* and the appreciation of the context and background of *gomei* are major aspects of the appeal of chanoyu in the modern world.

TABLE OF CONTENTS　もくじ

SUMMER

秋

AUTUMN

WINTER

本書の使い方　How to use this book

茶の湯と切っても切り離せない関係にある「銘」。季節を大事にする心やおもてなしの気持ちが込められ、日本独自の習慣・行事も学べる「銘」は、英語で茶の湯を説明する際に最適なトピックです。本書では、茶席でよく使われる100種類の銘を季節ごとにバイリンガルで紹介しています。

◎銘は、主に俳句で用いられる「季語」である場合も多いため、季語としても扱われるものは黒括弧、季語ではないものは白抜きの括弧で表記しています。

【 *gomei* & a haiku season word **】** 〚 *gomei* & not a haiku season word 〛

◎季節は新暦を基本として、新年（1月）、春（2〜4月）、夏（5〜7月）、秋（8〜10月）、冬（11〜12月）の5章に分類しています。また、各季節の中で用いられる時期が限定される銘には、下記のようにその目安を表記しています。

[early season]　　　[middle season]　　　[late season]

初○　　　　　　仲○　　　　　　晩○

early　　　　　　mid　　　　　　late

◎銘をはじめとする日本語を英文中で表記する場合はイタリック体にしています。ただし人名や地名、また「chanoyu」「kimono」「haiku」など、すでに英語として定着している日本語については書体を変えていません。

新年

NEW YEAR'S

1月
Jan.

茶人の年中行事の最たるもののひとつが初茶
会です。一年の始まりを皆で華やかに、厳か
に祝い、心を新たにして互いの福寿を願いま
す。1月は季節の区切りとしては冬ですが、こ
こでは新年を寿ぐ代表的な銘を紹介します。

The Ceremony of the First Tea Gathering of the
New Year is one of the most important of the
annual events for tea practitioners. Everyone cele-
brates the beginning of the new year in a dignified
and resplendent manner. With a renewed spirit,
people mutually pray for long life and happiness.
The month of January is in the seasonal division of
winter, but representative *gomei* celebrating the
New Year are introduced separately here.

一月

〖曙〗

Akebono

夜が明けはじめる頃、さらに言えば新年最初の夜明けを
意味する。物事が新鮮で新しい時期である。曙棗という
玄々斎好みの棗がよく新年の茶会に用いられる。

Akebono means dawn or daybreak, and by extension, the first dawn and the beginning of the year
when things are fresh and new. The *Gengensai
konomi natsume* "*Gengensai* favored lacquered
thin tea container" called *Akebono* is often used
for tea gatherings during the New Year's season.

〖初夢〗

Hatsuyume

1月1日の夜、地域によっては2日の夜にみる、新年
初めての夢を意味する。宝船の絵を枕の下に入れて、
良い夢を祈願する習慣がある。縁起の良い夢として、
まず富士が、その次に鷹が、そしてその次に茄子があ
げられる（一富士二鷹三茄子）。これらは銘やあらゆる
茶道具に登場するモチーフになっている。

Hatsuyume is the first dream of the New Year
on the night of January 1st or in some places, the
2nd. It was the custom to put a picture of the
takarabune "treasure ship" under one's pillow
to ensure a good dream. It was thought that, in
order of auspiciousness, Mt. Fuji was first; a hawk,
second; and an eggplant, third. These appear as
motifs and poetic names for many tea utensils.

〘七福神〙
Shichifukujin

恵比須・大黒天・毘沙門天・弁財天・福禄寿・寿老人・布袋の七人の幸運の神のことで、しばしば宝船に乗った姿で描かれる。とても人気のあるモチーフで、七福神の持っている道具やその使者、それぞれの名前も銘などに登場する。

The Seven Gods of Good Fortune are Ebisu, Daikokuten, Bishamonten, Benzaiten, Fukurokuju, Jurojin and Hotei. They are often depicted as a group riding the *takarabune*. The *Shichifukujin* form a very popular design motif, and the gods are sometimes represented by their implements or their messengers, and their names also appear separately as *gomei*, as well.

〘来復〙
Raifuku

「一陽来復」(「陽」がまた来る)という語句の一部分。『易経』によると、陰が極まったのち、陽が増え始めるという。これは新年が来る、または春が再びやって来るということも意味する。来復は、悪い事が続いた後、ついに幸運に向かうことを暗示している。

Raifuku is part of the phrase "*ichiyo raifuku* (one *yo* [yang] returns)." According to *The Book of Changes*, when the *in* (*yin*) is completely exhausted, the *yo* will begin to increase. It can also mean that the New Year has come or that spring has returned. *Raifuku* implies that after a bad spell, things are finally beginning to turn around.

【七草】
Nanakusa

春に採れる七種の薬草をさす。これらを七草粥にして1月7日の朝に食べ、健康や繁栄を祈願する。セリ、ナズナ、ゴギョウ、ハコベラ、ホトケノザ、スズナ、スズシロの七草。

Haru no nanakusa are the seven herbs of spring. These are eaten in *nanakusa-gayu* "rice gruel" on the morning of January 7th to pray for good health and prosperity. The seven herbs are *seri* "Japanese parsley," *nazuna* "shepherd's purse," *gogyo* "cotton weed," *hakobera* "common chickweed," *hotokenoza* "lamium amplexicaule," *suzuna* "turnip," and *suzushiro* "daikon radish."

【宝船】
Takarabune

「宝船」は、七福神を神話に登場する「蓬莱山」からこの世界へと連れてくる宝の船のこと。しばしば宝物や七福神、米俵がいっぱいに載った様子が描かれる。帆にはよく「宝」という漢字が書かれている。

The treasure ship transports the Seven Gods of Good Fortune from the mythical Mt. Horai to this world. The ship is depicted with the seven gods riding on the deck, piled high with the lucky treasures (*takaramono*) or loaded with rice bales. The sail is often depicted with the Chinese character for treasure (宝) on it.

〔**末広**〕

Suehiro

扇のこと。要^{かなめ}から外側に開いていることから、永遠につきない幸運の象徴とされる。扇子の形や開く過程を描いたデザインはさまざまな道具や着物などに登場する。

Suehiro is a fan, which symbolizes ever-increasing good fortune because it opens outward from the pivot pin. The motif of a fan, open or in various stages of opening, appears on scrolls, many kinds of tea utensils, and kimono, etc.

〔**瑞雲**〕

Zuiun

吉兆を予言する雲。この雲は青・黄・赤・白・黒の五色で、甘露の雨を降らせる。中国では、瑞雲は皇帝の徳を褒め称える現象といわれる。この現象は太陽の近くにある薄い雲の水滴の間を太陽光が通りぬける時に生じ、鮮やかに雲を彩る。類義語に「慶雲」「紫雲」「彩雲」がある。

Zuiun are clouds which foretell auspicious events or happenings. It is said that the clouds appear in five colors—blue, yellow, red, white and black—and produce sweet rain. In China, it was a phenomenon honoring or praising the virtues of the emperor. This phenomenon occurs when sunlight passes through water droplets in thin clouds that appear near the sun and produces beautiful colors on them. Related words are *keiun* "auspicious clouds," *shiun* "purple clouds," or *saiun* "iridescent clouds."

銘とは何か

銘を学ぶのは、とても楽しいことです。なぜなら、茶道を学びはじめた人が最初に出合うものだからです。例えば、お茶のお稽古に行けば、必ず銘がつけられたお菓子が出されることでしょう。「旬」という言葉はもともと10日間毎の初日という意味で、新鮮であること、食べごろであること、最新であること、さらにいえば流行していること、人気であることを表しています。一般的に、季節の名前がつけられたお菓子は、だいたい10日くらいの間に提供され、次のものへと切り替わります。和菓子はたった4つか5つの基本的な技術を用いて作られるので、常に新しく、そして季節に合う和菓子をつくるために、色や形、銘が変えられるのです。菓銘は実際にその現象が起きる時や最盛期を迎える時より前に使われ、現象が終わった後には使えません。例えば、「桜」という銘のお菓子は桜が咲く前に使われ、舞い散った花びらを表現する場合を除いては、桜が散った後には使えないのです。

季節の銘は茶杓にもつけられます。亭主は点前が終わると薄茶器や茶杓といった道具を客に出し、客により近くで見てもらえるようにします。そして亭主が道具を持って帰る前に、正客が作者と銘を尋ねます。客は銘から亭主がその席に込めた思いや、微妙な季節の変化を感じることができるのです。

銘を学ぶには、季語を列挙した本を読むのが手軽です。こうした本は「歳時記」と呼ばれます。もともと、歳時記は俳句をつくる人のための本でした。俳句には必ず季語を入れなければならないので、季語の意味を解説する辞書や一覧表がつくられたのです。歳時記ではそれぞれの季語について、俳句の例や関連語、同義語が掲載されています。最近の歳時記は写真が豊富ですし、インターネットには言葉や例句を検索できる機能がついたサイトがあります。

What are *Gomei*
"Poetic Names"?

Learning about *gomei* "poetic names" can be very enjoyable, because they are encountered from the very beginning of chanoyu study. For example, each time a student goes to *keiko* "practice," she will be served *wagashi* "Japanese sweets" that almost always have *gomei*. Originally, The word *shun* or *jun* means the first day of a ten-day period and has alternate meanings of fresh, in season, up to date, and by extension, popular or in vogue. Generally, a seasonally named sweet appears for about ten days and then changes. Since *wagashi* are made using only four or five basic techniques, the color, shape, and poetic names are changed periodically to keep their references up to date and appropriate for the season. The *gomei* of a sweet usually refers to an upcoming or future phenomenon and is not used after that phenomenon has ended. For example, sweets referring to *sakura* "cherry blossom" are used up until the time the flowers bloom, but not after the flowers have fallen, unless it refers to the scattered or fallen flowers.

Another example of *gomei* are the names given to *chashaku* "tea scoops." After the host has finished the *temae* "tea procedure," he puts out the *chashaku* along with the *usuchaki* "thin tea container" for the guests to look at up close. Before removing them from the tea room, the main guest asks about the person who carved the *chashaku* and gave it its *gomei*. From the *gomei*, the guests are able to appreciate the attention that the host has put into the gathering and how he has selected a *chashaku* to be in harmony with the season.

In order to make the study of *gomei* easier, there are books that list words according to the season. These are called *saijiki* "almanac of poetic words and phrases." Originally, *saijiki* were books compiled for writers of haiku poetry. By convention each haiku verse was required to use a *kigo* "seasonal word," and dictionaries or lists were compiled listing the words and giving the meanings and period when they could be used. The *saijiki* also gave sample haiku and related or different words for each entry. Nowadays, modern *saijiki* feature photos to illustrate the entries, and the internet has sites which feature search functions for words and poems.

歳時記において、季語はふつう旧暦をもとに立項されています。四季ごとに分けられ、さらにいえば初春・仲春・晩春といったように、1つの季節が3つの部分に分けられています。それとは別に正月の季語の項があり、また季節を問わない無季の項が特別に設けられている場合もあります。

俳句のための季語を集めることからはじまった歳時記ですが、今や和菓子や茶花、取り合わせ、懐石など、茶の湯を色々な切り口で勉強する際に適した歳時記がたくさんあります。また茶道具の銘を紹介する茶の湯専用の辞書や用語集もありますし、茶人に向けたカレンダーの多くに二十四節気（102頁参照）や日ごと・週ごと・月ごとの銘が掲載されています。

銘や季語を勉強することで、理解が深まり視野が広がります。万葉の頃から、日本人は季節の変化をよく観察して味わい、芸術や文学の中で季節をいとおしむ気持ちを表現し、各季節の美しさを知っている唯一の民族だと考えるようになりました。世界で日本だけが四季があると考える人もいます。もはや日本が他のどの地域よりもはっきりとした季節の違いがあるわけではありませんが、千年以上培われてきた文化的背景からそのような誤解が生まれるのです。日本人に聞いても、伝統的な暦で現在がどの季節なのか答えられる人は少ないでしょう。

The words are usually listed according to the old lunar calendar. There are four sections for each of the seasons, and each season is divided into three parts, early, middle, and late, for example, *soshun* "early spring," *chushun* "middle spring," and *banshun* "late spring." Usually there is a separate section for *Shogatsu* "New Year's." Sometimes there was also a special section for *muki* "non-seasonal words."

Although originally a compilation of *kigo* for haiku, *saijiki* are now written for specific aspects of chanoyu study, for example, *wagashi*, *chabana* "flowers for the tea room," *toriawase* "assemblage of tea utensils," and *kaiseki* "chanoyu cuisine." There are also dictionaries or glossaries containing *gomei* of objects specifically used in chanoyu. Calendars for chanoyu practitioners often have the *Nijushi Sekki* "24 Point Seasonal Days" (see Column 3, page 70 for more detailed information) and a list of *gomei* for each day, week, or month.

By studying *gomei*, a whole new dimension of appreciation is opened. From the Man'yo Period (second half of 8th century), the Japanese have observed and appreciated the changing of the seasons and expressed that love in many forms of art and literature, leading to the idea that awareness of the beauties of nature in each season is a specifically Japanese attribute. There is also the idea that in the entire world, only Japan has four distinct seasons. The seasons are no more distinct and discernible here than in any other location, but this accumulated cultural background from over 1,000 years leads to this fallacy. If asked, the average Japanese person probably could not tell what season it was by the traditional reckoning or by the ever-changing weather.

SPRING

2月 — 4月

Feb. — Apr.

春というには寒すぎるも、暦の上では春を迎える2月。文字通り、季節の分かれ目である節分を機に、茶席の取り合わせは一気に春の装いに変わります。梅と桜に彩られ、徐々に夏へと向かう瑞々しい銘を取り上げます。

According to the calendar, February welcomes spring, although having said that, it is still far too cold. From *Setsubun*–as the word indicates, the day dividing the season–the *toriawase* "assemblage of tea utensils" for tea gatherings changes all at once to the adornment of springtime. Fresh and vibrant *gomei*, tinted by *ume* and sakura and gradually advancing toward summer, are featured.

二月
｜
四月

〔芳春〕

Hoshun

香り高い春のこと。花が咲き誇る、春のさかりのこと。無数の花から漂う芳香が、春の大気に満ち、私たちの心を満たす。

Hoshun means fragrant spring. The flowers are in full bloom, and it is the peak of springtime. The fragrance of myriad flowers perfumes the spring air and lifts our spirits.

〔下萌〕

Shitamoe

初春
○
early

枯草や雪の下から芽吹く植物のこと。不毛な土地の中で、植物は若芽を伸ばしはじめ、土中から芽を出す。厳しい冬を乗り越え、春の訪れとともに復活する植物の強さを感じることができる。関連する句に、藤原家隆 (1158~1237) の有名な和歌からとられた「雪間の草」がある。

Shitamoe means plants sprouting under last year's dried grasses or under the snow. In the barren fields, plants begin to send forth new green shoots that push through the ground. We can feel the strength of the plants that have endured the severe winter and are now coming back to life with the arrival of spring. A related phrase is *yukima no kusa* "green shoots amidst the snow" from a well-known poem by Fujiwara Ietaka (1158 – 1237).

〔花の兄〕 *Hana no ani*

初春
○
early

文字通り花（桜）の兄という意味で、梅をさす。司馬炎（236~290）は学問を愛したが、彼が学問をしていると梅の花が咲き、終えるとしぼんだといわれている。これが「好文木」という別名のゆえんである。梅は「此花」「春告草」とも呼ばれる。梅は冬の雪のなかで開花し美しい香りを放つため、美と清浄、また忍耐と希望の象徴である。松、竹と共に歳寒三友の一つで、蘭、菊、竹と共に四君子の一つである。

Hana no ani literally means elder brother of the flowers (cherry blossoms) and refers to the Japanese apricot (*ume* / prunus mume). In China it was said that the *ume* flowers bloomed when the scholarly Emperor Wu of Jin (236 – 290) studied and closed when he finished. This is the origin of an alternate name for *ume*, *kobunboku* "literature-loving tree." The *ume* is also called *konohana* and *harutsugegusa* "spring-announcing plant." Because the *ume* blooms amidst the snow and gives off a beautiful fragrance, it symbolizes perseverance and hope, as well as beauty and purity. It is one of the Three Friends of Winter (*shochikubai*) with the pine and bamboo, and one of the Four Gentlemen (*shikunshi*) with the orchid, chrysanthemum, and bamboo.

〖福は内〗

Fuku wa uchi

初春
○
early

幸福は家の中へ、という意味。節分（2月3日か4日頃。冬と春を分ける日）に、宮中では追儺（ついな）の式が開かれ、赤、緑、黒の鬼が象徴する悪霊を追い払う。庶民の間で、「福は内、鬼は外」と唱えながら炒り豆を投げる豆まきの風習がおこった。この儀式を行うことで、春の最初の日（立春）を迎えられる。ふっくらした頬で描かれる女性・お多福は、福が多いと書く名前のために、幸福を具現化したモチーフとしてよく用いられる。「節分」は冬の季語だが、現在茶の湯では2月に用いられることが多い銘のため、初春のことばとして挙げた。

Fuku wa uchi means good fortune comes into the home. On *Setsubun* (February 3rd or 4th, the dividing day between winter and spring), *Tsuina no shiki* "the rite of exorcism" was held at court to dispel evil spirits, which were represented by red, green and black *oni* "demons." Among the commoners, there arose the custom of *mamemaki* "scattering beans," which involved throwing roasted beans while chanting, "*Fuku wa uchi, oni wa soto*" (good fortune comes into the home; the *oni* demons go out). With this ritual, people welcomed the first day of spring. *Otafuku* (a woman depicted with fat cheeks) is often seen as an embodiment of good fortune because her name can be written with the characters for "much good fortune." *Setsubun* is a seasonal word for winter, but in chanoyu it is quite often used as a *gomei* in February, so it is included with early spring *gomei*.

【懸想文】 *Keso-bumi* 初春
○
early

恋文のこと。後に、恋文に似せてつくられた良縁や夫婦円満、商売繁盛のお札をさす言葉となった。元禄期、元日から 15 日、赤い袴と烏帽子を身に付け、白い布で顔を覆った懸想文売りが京都でこのお札を売り歩いた。

Keso-bumi means a love letter, but the word later came to refer to a talisman to pray for good fortune in finding a good match, ensuring marital happiness, and cultivating business prosperity. During the Genroku Period (1688 – 1704), from the first until the fifteenth of the new year, *kesobumi uri* (sellers of these talismans), wearing red *hakama* "formal divided skirt," *tate eboshi* "standing black hat," and a white face covering, wandered throughout Kyoto selling these charms.

〔東風〕

Kochi

東から吹く春の風をさした上品で詩的な言葉である。
春一番と呼ばれる春に初めて吹く風とは違い、寒さ
の残る中に吹く荒い東風はしばしば雨をともなう。東
風が雪を溶かし、梅を開花させ、それによって春の
訪れを告げると言われている。有名な学者で歌人の
菅原道真（845〜903）は、大宰府へ左遷された際に京
都の自宅の庭にある梅について次のような歌を詠んだ。

　　東風吹かばにほひおこせよ梅の花
　　主なしとて春な忘れそ

東風は他の語と組み合わせて「朝東風」「雨東風」
「梅東風」などと使われることもある。

Kochi is an elegant poetic word that refers to the spring wind
that blows from the east. Unlike the first wind of spring called
haru-ichiban, there is a lingering chill in this rough wind, which
is often accompanied by rain. It is said to melt the snow, to
cause the *ume* to bloom, and, thereby, to announce the arrival
of spring. Sugawara Michizane (845 – 903), the famous scholar
and poet, wrote the following poem about the *ume* in his garden
in Kyoto after he was relegated to Dazaifu, "When the east wind
blows, flourish in full bloom, you plum blossoms, even though
you lose your master, don't be oblivious to spring." Kochi appears
in combination with other words, *asa-gochi* "morning *kochi*,"
ame-gochi "rain *kochi*," *ume-gochi* "apricot *kochi*," etc.

〔春告鳥〕 *Harutsugedori*

春を告げる鳥のことで、ウグイスをさす。日本の和歌によく出てくるモチーフで、現存する最古の和歌集『万葉集』(759 年頃編) に登場する。ウグイスはよく梅と取りあわされ、お互いを想起させる関係である。ウグイスの歌は際立って美しく、ウグイスの鳴き声をさした初音（春の最初の歌）という語がある。

Harutsugedori means spring-announcing bird and refers to the *uguisu* "Japanese bush warbler (Horornis diphone)." It is a favorite subject of Japanese poetry and was featured in the *Man'yoshu* (compiled ca. 759), the oldest extant collection of Japanese *waka*. The *uguisu* is so often featured with *ume* that mentioning one will conjure up the other. The song of the *uguisu* is particularly beautiful, and the poetic word *hatsune* "first song" in spring refers to the song of the *uguisu*.

【早蕨】

Sawarabi

仲春
○
mid

わらびの新芽のこと。日当たりの良い山腹に芽を出す
わらびの芽は食べることができ、春を代表する存在
である。多年生のシダで、日本中で芽を出す。新芽
は渦巻き状で、よくデザインのモチーフになる。野菜
として食べられるほか、根を乾かし、粉にしてつくっ
たデンプンでわらび餅というお菓子もつくられる。
わらび餅は年中食べられるが、特に春に人気である。

Sawarabi means new bracken shoot (Pteridium aquilinum). Appearing in sunny places on mountainsides, the edible *warabi* shoots are representative of spring. It is a perennial fern and grows throughout Japan. The new shoots have a fiddlehead shape, which often appears as a design motif. It is eaten as a vegetable, and starch made from its dried and powdered roots is used to make a sweet called *warabi mochi*, which is enjoyed all year long, but is especially appropriate in the spring.

【淡雪】

Awayuki

軽く雪が降ること。春の小雪は、水分とあたたかい気温
のために非常に解けやすい。雪片が大きく、「ぼたん雪」
と呼ばれる塊になりやすい。春の雪は、降りつもること
なく解けてしまう侘しさがある。立春（2月4日頃）のあ
とに降る雪は「春の雪」「春雪」と呼ばれる。

Awayuki means light snowfall. The light snow in spring melts very easily because of its wetness and warming temperatures. The snowflakes are large and easily form clusters called *botan yuki* "snow peony." There is a poignancy in the spring snow that melts without ever forming drifts. Snow that falls after *risshun* "the first day of spring" (around February 4th) is called *haru no yuki* or *shunsetsu*.

【雛の宴】　*Hina no en*　仲春
○
mid

文字通りいえば人形の宴のことで、雛祭りの人形飾りの前で食べるお祝いの食事をさす。元々は上巳（3月の初巳の日）と呼ばれる禊の儀式としてはじまったもので、江戸時代（1603~1867）にそれが桃の節供と呼ばれる五節句のうちの一つとなった。雛棚の上に、桃の花、三色で菱形の餅菓子である菱餅、白酒というノンアルコールの甘酒が用意される。ぼんぼりの灯は夕方前にともされ、家族の、特に女性が女の子の成長と発達を願う。かつては、宮廷で和歌の会も一緒に開かれていたという。

Hina no en literally means doll banquet, and refers to a celebratory meal eaten in front of the display of dolls for *Hina matsuri* "the Doll Festival." Originally held as a rite of purification called *joshi* "first snake day of the third month," in the Edo Period (1603 – 1867), it became the second of the Five Feast Days (*Gosekku*) called *Momo no sekku,* or "peach festival." Peach flowers, *hishimochi* "tricolored, diamond-shaped *mochi* sweets," and *shirazake* "white sake, a non-alcoholic rice drink," are offered on the *hina-dana* "stand for the dolls." The *bonbori* "lamps" are lit in the late afternoon, and the family, particularly the female members, gather to pray for the growth and development of the girls of the family. In the olden days, the *hina no en* was observed in the court with poetry writing parties.

春

二月—四月

【春雨】
Harusame

春に降る細かな雨のこと。ふつう、強い季節風が吹く合間の時期で、大雨がなく、風が穏やかになる頃に降る。3月や4月に細かい雨が降り続くことで、草木は芽吹き、花が咲き、春の特別な趣がもたらされる。詩歌において、春雨は「催花雨」ともいわれる。

Harusame means fine spring rain. It normally occurs between the periods of strong seasonal winds, when there are no heavy rains, and the winds are calmer. The fine, continuously falling rain, common in March and April, accompanies the special charms of the spring season; it causes the buds of leaves and plants to swell and the flowers to bloom. In poetry it is also called *saikau* "the rain that hastens the flowers to bloom."

【朧月】
Oborozuki

かすんだ月のこと。春は湿度が高く、日中霞が生じる。日が暮れるにつれ、暖かい春の夜はやわらかく包みこむようで、あらゆるものの輪郭や色、姿をなだらかに、ぼんやりとさせる。春の月はぼんやりとかすんで見えることが多く、朧月や月朧と呼ばれる。関連語に、朧月夜や春朧がある。

Oborozuki means hazy moon. In the spring there is much moisture in the air, and mist forms during the day. As the evening deepens, the warm spring night takes on a soft, enveloping feeling, which makes the outline, color, and appearance of everything gentle and indistinct. The spring moon usually appears faint and blurry and is called *oborozuki* or *tsuki-oboro*. Related words include *oborozukiyo* "night of the hazy moon" and *haru-oboro* "spring indistinctness."

〖初燕〗

Hatsutsubame

仲春
—○—
mid

その年最初の燕のこと。春の中頃、燕は南方か
ら日本各地へ戻ってきて、人家の軒下に巣をつ
くって子育てをする。最初の燕を見るということ
は、春の盛りが近いということを意味する。燕は
幸運をもたらすとされ、燕が巣をつくった家は繁
栄する、豊作が続く、子孫繁栄する、火事が起
こらない、病気にならないなどといわれる。

Hatsutsubame means the first swallow of that year. In
the middle part of spring, swallows return from the south
to every region of Japan and build nests under the eaves
of houses to raise their families. Seeing the first swallow
means that the height of spring is near. Swallows are
thought to bring good fortune. Homes where swallows
build their nests will prosper; good harvests will ensue; the
family will have many descendants; homes will be protect-
ed from fires; and illnesses will be prevented.

〔佐保姫〕

Sao-hime

佐保山と佐保川の女神で、春の山野をつかさどる。東は春の方角で、佐保山と佐保川はかつての都、平城京（現在の奈良）の東に位置していた。佐保姫は霧の衣を織り、柳の細い枝を緑に染め、梅の花笠を編み、桜の花を咲かせるという。一方、秋の女神は龍田姫で、かつての都の西に位置する龍田山と龍田川をつかさどる。現在、佐保川の土手に5キロメートルにわたって桜が植えられており、「奈良県景観資産」と名づけられている。

Sao-hime is the goddess of Mt. Saho and the Saho River, who rules over the fields and mountains during spring. The east is the direction of spring, and these two features were located to the east of the ancient capital of Heijokyo (present-day Nara). Sao-hime is said to weave garments of mist, to dye the slender branches of the willow green, to weave hats of *ume* flowers, and to cause the cherry blossoms to bloom. In contrast, the goddess of autumn Tatsuta-hime reigns over Mt. Tatsuta and the Tatsuta River to the west of the ancient capital. Today the banks of the Saho River have been planted with *sakura* trees for five kilometers and are named a "Landscape Asset of Nara."

〔山笑う〕

Yamawarau

文字通りにいえば山が笑うという意味で、春の山の木々が若芽を伸ばし、花を咲かせている様子を元気に笑っていると擬人化している。この言葉は、中国の北宋の画家、郭熙（1020~90 頃）の詩、「春山淡冶にして笑うが如く、夏山蒼翠にして滴るが如く、秋山明浄にして粧うが如く、冬山惨淡として眠るが如し」に由来する。植物が芽吹いて、冬枯れのどんよりとした茶色がゆっくりと明るくなり、山々は人のように笑っている。

Yamawarau literally means the mountains laugh. The spring mountains are personified and are seen as smiling cheerfully when trees are sending out new leaves and flowers are blooming. The phrase comes from a Chinese painter of the North Song dynasty, Guo Xi (Jpn. Kaku Ki, ca.1020 – 90), who wrote, "The spring mountains are captivatingly pale, just as if they were smiling; the summer mountains are lushly green, just as if they were overflowing with freshness; the autumn mountains are perfectly clear, just as if they were dressed up; the winter mountains are pitiably sad, just as if they were dead." The dull brown colors of winter slowly turn bright as the shoots of the plants appear, and the mountains, if they were human, would be smiling.

〔帰雁〕

Kigan

仲春
———
mid

帰っていく雁のこと。日本で冬を越すために南下して
きた雁は、春に北へ帰って行く。空を飛ぶ雁の美し
さと悲しげな鳴き声から、渡り鳥の中でも雁はよく歌
のテーマとなる。今ではマガンやヒシクイ、サカツラ
ガンが最も一般的に見られる。

Kigan means returning geese. The geese that came south in the autumn to pass the winter in Japan return to the north in the spring.
Because of the beauty of the geese in flight and the plaintive sound
of their cries, they are the favorite migratory bird to be used as poetry
themes. These days, the greater white-fronted goose, the bean goose,
and the swan goose are commonly seen.

【花筏】

Hanaikada

晩春
———
late

花の筏のことで、川面にまとまって落ちて流れる桜の
花びらを筏にたとえたことば。意匠としては、流れる
水を背景として、丸太でできた筏の上に花もしくは枝
つきの花が描かれる。落ちる花びらの穢れのない美
と無常が心に刻まれる。

Hanaikada means flower raft and
likens the fallen cherry blossom petals, flowing in a mass down streams
and rivers, to a raft. As an art motif,
this design usually features flowers, or
branches with flowers, on a raft of logs
with flowing water in the background.
The unsullied beauty and transiency of the falling petals is etched in people's hearts.

〔野遊び〕

Noasobi

晩春
——
late

野山を楽しむために出かけること。元々、春の農作業に入る前の農民が、田の神の祝福を受けるために身を清め、山に登っていた。この習慣が、後につくしやわらび、よもぎといった春の植物をとりながら草木や春の花の中を歩き、厳しい寒さの後のあたたかな気候を味わうなど、素晴らしい春の気候を楽しむ遊びとなっていった。関連する他の語に、「山遊び」や「春遊び」、「野掛け」がある。

Noasobi means going out to enjoy the fields and mountains. Originally, before beginning agricultural activities in the spring, farmers went up into the mountains to purify themselves in order to receive the blessings of the god of the rice fields. Later, this became a pleasure outing to enjoy the fine spring weather by picking spring plants, such as *tsukushi* "horsetail," *warabi* "bracken," and *yomogi* "Japanese mugwort," to walk amidst the greenery and spring flowers, and to enjoy the warm weather after the harsh winter. Other related words are *yama-asobi* "mountain enjoyment," *haru-asobi* "spring enjoyment" and *nogake* "going out to enjoy the fields."

〔長閑〕

Nodoka

平和で穏やかなこと。また、太陽にやわらかく照らされた春の日のゆったりとくつろいだ気持ちのこと。日が長くなっていき、時間がゆっくりと過ぎるように感じられる。

Nodoka means peaceful and tranquil, and refers to the feeling of ease and relaxation when the sun softly illuminates a spring day. The days become longer, and time seems to pass by slowly.

〔春の野〕 *Haru no no*

春の野原のこと。田んぼの畦道、小川の土手、山の斜面に
植物は芽吹き、無数の花が開く。鳥は春の日差しの中で歌い、
すがすがしい風が吹く。山の陰には雪が残るも、暖かな陽光、
スミレやタンポポ、トクサ、ワラビの芽が枯れ草の間からち
らりと顔をのぞかせる。

Haru no no means spring fields. On raised footpaths
between rice paddies, on embankments of streams and
rivers, and on the mountain slopes, plants are sprouting, and myriad flowers are blooming. Birds are singing
in the spring sunshine and the refreshing breeze. In the
shadows of the mountains, lingering snow is seen, but
in the warm sunlight, violets, dandelions, horsetails, and
bracken shoots are peeking through the dried grasses on
the ground.

〔吉野山〕　*Yoshinoyama*　晩春
── ○
late

奈良県の吉野山のことで、『古今和歌集』(905 年頃成立) に詠まれた当時から桜で有名である。修験道の開祖である役行者 (7 世紀後半) が、修験道の本尊、蔵王権現の像を桜の木に彫って吉野山に祀ったと伝えられ、それを機に霊場参拝者が桜の木を山の斜面に植えはじめた。3 万本の桜の木が植えられているといわれ、吉野という言葉だけでも山に咲いている桜が想起される。吉野山には天皇が何度も訪れ、第 96 代の後醍醐天皇 (在位 1318~39) は吉野に朝廷を置いた。その頃から多くの遺跡があり、一帯が世界遺産に登録されている。

Yoshinoyama refers to Mt. Yoshino in Nara Prefecture that was famous for its *sakura* "cherry trees" from the time it was first mentioned in a poem featured in the *Kokin Wakashu* (published ca. 905). The founder of *Shugendo* (mountain asceticism) En no Gyoja (latter part of the 7th century) is said to have carved a statue of Zao Gongen, the most important deity of the sect, from cherry wood and enshrined it at Mt. Yoshino. Because of that, pilgrims began to plant cherry trees on the slopes of the mountain. It is said that there are 30,000 cherry trees planted there, and just the mention of Yoshino conjures images of cherry trees blooming in the mountains. It was the destination of many imperial visits, and the 96th Emperor, Go-Daigo (reign 1318 – 39), established his court there. There are many historic sites from that period, and the whole area has been designated an UNESCO World Heritage site.

〔百千鳥〕　*Momochidori*

無数の鳥のこと。空が明るくなり、数々の鳥がさえずり始める春の夜明けのイメージ。また、その名の通り、数え切れない千鳥のこともさす。平安後期から室町時代にかけては、この言葉は鶯を意味していたが、のちに一種類だけでなく、あらゆる小さな鳥を総称する言葉となった。

Momochidori means myriad birds. The image is of spring dawn when the sky begins to brighten and many varieties of birds begin to sing. As the name indicates, it also referred to countless plovers (*chidori*). From the late Heian Period until the Muromachi Period (from the late 12th century until the 15th century), the word was used to mean the *uguisu* "bush warbler," but later it was used to indicate not just plovers, but all little birds inclusively.

〔藤波〕
Fujinami

晩春
—○—
late

晩春、薄紫の花の房が長く垂れ下がって全体を覆う。風が吹くと、房が優しく前や後ろへ揺れ動く、その美しい様子を藤波と呼ぶ。古くから藤は鉢で育てられるか、房や花を観賞するため棚で育てられてきた。山の斜面で多様に咲き誇る自然のままの藤はさながら滝のようである。

Fujinami means wisteria waves. In the late spring the plant is covered with long, hanging clusters of light purple flowers. When the wind blows, the clusters sway gently back and forth, and this beautiful sight is called *fujinami*. From long ago wisteria plants have been grown in pots or trained to grow on a trellis to show off the clusters of flowers. In the mountains the blooming wild variety growing on a hillside resembles a waterfall.

〔花吹雪〕
Hanafubuki

晩春
—○—
late

花の吹雪のこと。桜が開花し、散り始めるまでの期間は非常に短く、散りゆく花びらの素晴らしく見事な情景をこの句はとらえている。南より吹いてくる風が、まさに吹雪のように花を空からとめどなく降り落とす。関連する言葉に「飛花」、「落花」、「花の塵」がある。

Hanafubuki means flower blizzard. The period from when the *sakura* bloom until they begin to fall is very short, and this phrase captures the brilliant, splendid scene of the falling petals. Winds blowing from the south often cause a storm of petals falling from the sky like a blizzard. Related words are *hika* "flying flower (petals)," *rakka* "fallen flowers" and *hana no chiri* "flower dust."

〔花衣〕

Hana-goromo

晩春
———○
late

花の衣のことで、花見に行くために女性が着る美しい着物の
ことをさす。元禄期（1688~1704）、小袖とよばれる豪華な
着物が流行し、野外に花見に出かける際、小袖が華やかな
幕のように木につりさげられた。平安時代の宮中では、異な
る色の薄い着物を重ねて着る習慣（十二単）があり、赤い着
物の上に白い着物を重ねたものは桜襲と呼ばれた。この桜
襲のことを、花衣とも呼んだ。

Hana-goromo means flowery robes and refers to the
beautiful kimono women wore to go flower viewing.
During the Genroku Period (1688 – 1704), it was the fad
to wear gorgeous kimono called *kosode* "short sleeves,"
and during outdoor flower viewing parties, the *kosode*
were hung from the trees like gorgeous curtains. In the
court of the Heian Period (794 – 1185), the layering of
light kimono (*junihitoe*) of different colors developed, and
the combination called *sakura-gasane* featured a white
top kimono over a red under kimono. *Sakura-gasane* was
also called *hana-goromo*.

〔柳の糸〕　*Yanagi no ito*　晩春
——○
late

春の風に吹かれて揺れている柳の、すらっとした若枝の美しさを表現した言葉。柳は生命力に満ち溢れ、春に新芽を出す最初の植物の一つである。古来、柳は長寿と繁栄をもたらす不思議な力を持つ神聖な木とされてきた。新芽の柳は「芽張柳」や「芽吹柳」と呼ばれる。

Yanagi no ito means willow thread and refers to the beauty of the slender new branches of the willow swaying in the spring breeze. The willow overflows with life force and is one of the first plants to send out green shoots in the spring. From ancient times the willow was considered a sacred tree that possessed magical powers to provide long life and prosperity. Green willows were called *mebariyanagi* and *mebukiyanagi* "sprouting willow."

銘 の 種 類

茶の湯の世界では、茶入や茶碗、茶杓といった、抹茶に直接触れるような主要な道具には銘がつけられます。銘は道具をより魅力的にしますし、また銘からは道具の所有者の美意識や、知識、茶の湯の精神を知ることができます。

銘の出典は様々で、例えば以下のようなものからとられます。

- **文学** — 詩、小説、(中国や日本の) 哲学
- **芸能** — 能、狂言、歌舞伎など
- **伝承** — 伝説、神話、民間伝承、寓話、物語
- **有名な歴史上の人物** — 公家、僧侶、武士、茶人、詩人
- **場所や地理的特色** — 山 (富士山など)、川、海岸、景勝地
- **季節的な現象** — 気象、天文、植物
- **日々の出来事** — 習俗、儀式、祭

このように様々なものから銘がつけられているという事実は、茶人が単に知識のレベルが高かっただけではなく、多くの異なった文化活動に関わり、交流していたことを示しています。かつて茶人には貴族や大名、神官、僧侶、豪商などがいたため、彼らが茶の湯の世界にもたらした知識や様々な視点は、銘やその関連知識の多大なる出所となりました。茶の湯は 500 年以上もの歴史があり、その歴史の中で道具に銘をつける習慣は高度に発達し、洗練され、また銘の元となる多くの知識が共有されてきました。

Types of *Gomei*
"Poetic Names"

In the world of chanoyu, *gomei* "poetic names" are given to major objects, such as thick tea containers, tea bowls, and tea scoops—objects that come into direct contact with the *matcha* "powdered green tea." These *gomei* enhance the objects and express the owner's aesthetic sensibility, erudition, and chanoyu spirit.

Gomei may come from many different sources, such as the following:

> **Literature** — poetry, novels, philosophy (both Chinese and Japanese)
> **Performing arts** — noh, kyogen, kabuki, etc.
> **Traditional lore** — legends, myths, folk tales, fables, stories
> **Famous historical personages** — nobles, priests, warriors, *chajin* "tea masters," poets
> **Places and geographic features** — mountains (e.g. Mt. Fuji), rivers, beaches, scenic spots
> **Seasonal occurrences** — weather phenomenon, astronomy, botany
> **Everyday life** — customs, observances, festivals

That these names have been taken from such diverse sources indicates not just the high level of general knowledge that the *chajin* possessed, but also the connectedness and cross-fertilization of many different cultural activities. Because *chajin* included members of the nobility, military leaders, priests and monks, and wealthy merchants, the knowledge and different viewpoints that they brought to the tea world provided a plethora of sources for names and references. Also, the fact that the tea world has a history of over 500 years means that the custom of giving *gomei* to objects has become highly developed and refined, and that there is a large shared background from which to draw.

名前がつけられた茶道具として早い例は「初花」と呼ばれる大名物茶入です。中国から伝来した茶入で、将軍の足利義政（1436~90）が名づけました。その後、織田信長（1534~82）と豊臣秀吉（1537~98）、徳川家康（1542~1616）という三人の天下人の手を渡りました。その名の通り、この茶入の洗練された美しさは早春に咲く花を想起させます。『古今和歌集』（905年頃成立）の歌からとられた名前と考えられています。

樂道入の手になる黒茶碗につけられた「獅子」という銘には、こんな面白い話があります。この銘は、清涼山という山にある石橋に来た寂昭法師の話を描いた能の演目「石橋」に由来します。橋の向こうは文殊菩薩の浄土です。文殊菩薩の使いである獅子が現れ、牡丹の花の中で踊ります。黒い茶碗にある白い文様が長い橋を思わせ、それがさらに踊る獅子を連想させます。

ある竹花入に「遅馬」という銘がつけられたように、茶人はユーモアのセンスも優れていたことがわかります。その花入には、壁や柱に掛けるために必要な穴がありませんでした。これが銘の中核をなす洒落を生み出したのです。「掛けられない」、つまり「駆けられない（=遅馬）」というわけです。

これら三つの例は、茶の湯における銘の豊かで美しい世界のほんの一端に過ぎません。

An early example of a named chanoyu object is the *omeibutsu* "grand object of renown" known as the *Hatsuhana* "First Flower" Chinese thick tea container that was named by the Shogun Ashikaga Yoshimasa (1436 – 1490). It was later owned by the three famous unifiers of Japan, Oda Nobunaga (1534 - 1582), Toyotomi Hideyoshi (1537 - 1598), and Tokugawa Ieyasu (1542 - 1616). The name refers to its refined beauty which suggests a flower blooming in the early spring. It is thought that the name came from a poem in the *Kokin Wakashu*.

An interesting *gomei* is one given to a black tea bowl made by Raku Donyu (also referred to as Nonko, 1599 – 1656) that is called *Shishi* "Lion." The name came from the noh play *Shakkyo* "Stone Bridge," which tells the story of a monk Jakusho who comes to a stone bridge across a deep gorge on Mt. Shoryozen. The land beyond the bridge is the Pure Land belonging to Manjusri Bodhisattva. A lion, the messenger of the Bodhi-sattva, appears and dances among the peonies. The black tea bowl has white markings that suggest the long arching bridge and by associa-tion, the dancing lion.

Chajin also had a keen sense of humor as seen in the *gomei* of a bam-boo vase called *Osouma* "Slow Horse." The container does not have a hole by which it can be hung on a wall or a pillar. This is the pun at the center of this name. The Japanese word *kakerarenai* "it cannot be hung" sounds like the word, with the same pronunciation, which means unable to run, hence the name "Slow Horse."

These three examples provide just a hint of the richness and beauty of the world of *gomei* in chanoyu.

SUMMER

———————————

5月 — 7月

May — Jul.

青葉の爽やかな季節、茶席の設えも炉から風炉へと様変わりし、茶人の夏がやってきます。じめじめとうっとうしい梅雨、また耐え難い酷暑の日々にも、日本の夏を伝える美しい言葉が茶会に楽しみを添えます。

When it is the season of fresh, green leaves, the equipment of the tearoom changes completely from *ro* "open hearth" to *furo* "brazier," and for tea people, summer has returned. During the humid and depressing rainy season and the unbearable, torrid days, the beautiful words that convey the Japanese summer add enjoyment and diversion to tea gatherings.

〔時鳥〕

Hototogisu

5月初句に南方から日本へやって来て、夏の始まり を告げる鳥。昔は時鳥の鳴き声と鶯の鳴き声を初音 と呼び待ちわびた。時鳥は人気の歌題で、『万葉集』 （759年頃成立）には153首、また『古今和歌集』（905 年頃成立）には42首がみられる。時鳥の鳴き声はふ つう橘と卯の花が咲く頃と同時期に聞こえるので、時 鳥とこれらの花を一緒に取り合わせることが多い。

Hototogisu is the lesser cuckoo that arrives in Japan from the south in early May and announces the beginning of summer. In the past, its singing was called *hatsune* "the first song (of summer)" and, like the song of the *uguisu* "bush warbler" in spring, it was much anticipated. *Hototogisu* was a popular theme for poetry in the *Man'yoshu* where it appeared in 153 poems and in the *Kokin Wakashu* where it appeared in 42 poems. The *hototogisu*'s song is usually heard around the same time when the *tachibana* "citrus *tachibana*" and *unohana* "deutzia" are in bloom, so the bird and these flowers were often grouped together.

〔薫風〕
Kunpu

初夏
—
early

芳しい風、微風のこと。爽やかなそよ風が新緑の中を抜け、咲き誇る花々の香りを運んでくる。初夏の青嵐（「せいらん」とも）と呼ばれる風より、優しく柔らかい風である。薫風は、中国の詩人・柳公権（778~865）が詠んだ詩の中の「薫風自南来　殿閣生微涼」（芳しい風が南より吹き来たり、宮殿に微かな涼しさが生まれる）という句に由来する。

Kunpu means fragrant wind or breeze. This refreshing breeze carries the scent of the many blooming flowers through the new green leaves of plants and trees. It is gentler and softer than the early summer wind called *aoarashi* or *seiran*. It comes from a phrase by the Chinese poet Liu Gongquan (778 – 865), "The fragrant wind comes from the south; a delicate coolness arises in the palace halls."

〔青嵐〕
Aoarashi
(Seiran)

新緑の季節に吹く強風をさす。『和漢朗詠集』（1017~21年頃成立）にある慶滋為雅の「夜極浦の波に宿すれば　青嵐吹いて皓月冷じ」（遠くの岸辺で青嵐が吹き、白々とした月が荒涼とあたりを照らしている）という和歌に登場する。

Aoarashi means green storm and refers to the strong wind which blows during the period of the new green leaves. The word appears in a poem in the *Wakan Ryoeishu* (Collection of Chinese and Japanese Poems, ca. 1017 – 21) by Yoshishige no Tamemasa about the green wind blowing and the bright, cold, white moon shining on the distant shore.

〔登鯉〕

Nobori-goi

初夏
○
early

のぼっていく鯉のこと。中国では、黄河上流の
瀧・龍門までのぼることができた鯉は、龍になる
という伝説がある。「鯉の瀧登り」「登龍門」は、
立身出世の象徴である。「男の子の日」とも呼ば
れる５月５日の端午の節句の飾りである鯉のぼ
りはこの句がもとになっている。端午の節句は、
五節句のうちのひとつである。

Nobori-goi means ascending
carp. In China, there is a legend that if a carp succeeds in
ascending the Dragon Gate,
a number of cataracts at the
headwaters of the Yellow
River, it will turn into a dragon. *Koi no takinobori* "carp
ascending the waterfall" and
toryumon "ascending to the
Dragon Gate" are used as
symbols of success in life. The phrase inspired the
carp streamers which are one of the decorations of
Tango no Sekku, often called "Boys' Day," which
occurs on May 5th. *Tango no Sekku* is one of the
Gosekku "Five Feast Days."

〔緑陰〕

Ryokuin

緑の影という意味で、新緑に日光がふりそそいででき
る影のことをさす。緑に囲まれた日陰で読書や昼寝を
したり、ピクニックをしたりするのはこの季節の楽し
みのひとつである。日中の木立の下の暗がりは「木下
闇」、木立の葉の間から漏れる日光のことを「木漏れ
日」という。

Ryokuin means green shadows and refers to the shadows
formed by the sunlight filtering through the new green
leaves. Activities such as reading, taking a nap, or having a
picnic in the verdant shade are some of the pleasures of the
season. The darkness under the trees during the day is called
konoshitayami and the sunlight filtering through the spaces
between the leaves in a grove of trees is called *komorebi*.

〔岩もる水〕

Iwamorumizu

苔むした岩や巨岩の間から豊かに湧き出て、深い森
の間を流れ落ちる水のこと。山の湧き水というよりも、
どちらかといえば地下から湧き出る水を「清水」もし
くは「真清水」と呼ぶ。ほかの類似語に「岩清水」、
「苔清水」、「山清水」がある。

Iwamorumizu means water gushing out profusely from
between moss-covered rocks and boulders and flowing down
through the deep forest. Water that flows out from the ground,
rather from a mountain spring, is called *shimizu* "pure water"
or *mashimizu* "very pure and clean water." Other similar words
are *iwa-shimizu* "fresh water from between the boulders,"
kokeshimzu "pure water amid the moss" and *yamashimizu*
"pure mountain water."

〔麦秋〕　*Bakushu*

文字通りには麦の秋という意味で、5 月から 6 月の、立派に
育った麦の穂が収穫される時期をさす。黄金の穂は日の光
の中で輝き、乾いた茎をなびかせながら麦畑を吹き抜ける
風が素晴らしい音を奏でる。通常雨が少なく乾燥した季節だ
が、間もなく梅雨に入るので、収穫時期は短い。

Bakushu literally means wheat autumn, and it refers
to the period in May and June when the ripened wheat
spikes are harvested. The golden spikes sparkle in the
sun, and the wind makes a wonderful sound as it blows
across the wheat fields rustling the dry stalks as it passes. Although there is not much rain during this dry period, the harvest season is short because the rainy season
begins soon afterward.

〔花菖蒲〕
Hanashobu

仲夏
—◦—
mid

花菖蒲は端午の節供の象徴。梅雨の頃、池や川の土手沿いに大きくて華やかな、紫と白の花が咲く。

Hanashobu is the Japanese iris (Iris ensata), which is the emblem of *Tango no sekku* (Boys' Day). Its large, gorgeous, purple and white flowers bloom along the banks of ponds and rivers around the time of the rainy season.

〔早苗〕
Sanae

仲夏
—◦—
mid

田んぼに植えるために準備されている稲の苗のこと。かつて、手作業で田植えが行われていた時は、苗を田んぼへ移す場面に関連した多くの言葉があった。例えば「苗打ち（苗の束を水を張った田に投げ込むこと）」や「早苗舟（苗を運ぶのに使った舟のこと）」、「早苗籠（早苗の入った籠のこと）」などがある。

Sanae means the seedlings of the rice plant that are prepared for planting in the paddies. In the past when rice planting was done by hand, there were many words related to the scene of the seedlings being transferred to the rice paddies, such as *nae-uchi* "bundles of seedlings thrown into the flooded rice fields," *sanaebune* "boats used to transport the seedlings" and *sanaekago* "seedling baskets."

〔蛍狩〕 *Hotaru-gari* 仲夏
—○—
mid

蛍を探しに出かけること。また、夏の夕べに清らかに流れる河川や小川の近くで涼をとること。かつては、川岸や田んぼをのんびりと歩き、蛍を見物したり捕まえたりするのが夏の風物詩だった。蛍は、薄い布や細い金網を張った木や竹の籠に入れられた。蛍売りと呼ばれる行商人が捕まえた蛍を売り歩いていた。蛍は落ちついた、明滅する光を放つ。また、有名な源氏蛍やそれより小さな平家蛍をはじめ、日本には 40 種類以上の蛍が確認されている。

Hotaru-gari means to go out in search of *hotaru* "fireflies" and to enjoy the coolness of summer evenings near streams and rivers with pure, flowing water. In the past people walking leisurely along the riverbanks and rice fields to watch or catch *hotaru* was a representative scene of summer. The *hotaru* were often put into wooden or bamboo-framed baskets, which were covered with thinly-woven cloth or fine metal net. Vendors called *hotaru uri* wandered the streets selling *hotaru* that they had caught. The *hotaru* give off a cool, flickering light, and there are over 40 types of fireflies in Japan with the *Genji-botaru* and smaller *Heike-botaru* being the best-known.

〔氷室〕

Himuro

晚夏
———○
late

氷の貯蔵室のこと。昔は、山でできた天然氷は地下室や洞穴などに夏まで蓄えられていた。夏まで氷を保存するために、茅やおがくずなどの断熱材が氷室に並べられた。夏の暑い中でも健康でいられるようにという祈りをこめて、氷室からの氷を天皇へ贈った。また江戸時代には将軍家にも贈られた。

Himuro means ice cellar. In the olden days, natural ice from the mountains was stored in cellars, caves, or pits until the summer. The *himuro* were lined with reeds, sawdust, and other insulation to preserve the ice until the summer. During the hot months, ice from the *himuro* was presented to the emperor and, later during the Edo Period (1603 – 1867), also to the shogun to pray for their good health during the heat of the summer.

〔夏木立〕

Natsukodachi

夏の木々のこと。木々はうっそうと茂る葉に包まれ、生命力みなぎる木々の陰は、ほっと息をつかせる場所である。「夏木立」は複数の木をさし、夏の一本の木のことは「夏木」という。

Natsukodachi means a stand of trees in the summer. The trees are covered with thick and luxuriant foliage, and in the shade of the trees, which overflows with life force, people find a place of safety and relaxation. The word refers to a grove or stand of trees, and *natsuki* refers to a single tree during this season.

〔茅の輪〕　*Chi no wa*　晩夏 —○ late

文字通りにはチガヤの輪という意味で、この植物の束で作った大きな輪のことをさす。6月の最後の日に、「夏越の祓」と呼ばれる行事の間、茅の輪が設置され、人々はこの輪の中を通り抜けて身を清め、無病息災を祈る。

Chi no wa means ring of cogon grass (Imperata cylindrica) and refers to a large wreath made of bundles of this grass. On the last day of the sixth month, during an observance called *Nagoshi no harae* "purification for passing the summer," *chi no wa* are erected at Shinto shrines and people pass through the large wreaths to purify themselves and to pray for good health and protection against disaster.

〔落し文〕 *Otoshi-bumi*

文字通りには落ちた手紙のことを意味し、オトシブミという昆虫が卵を産みつけるために丸めた葉のことをさす。丸めて落とされた葉が、恋人などに秘密のメッセージを伝えるために道端に落とす手紙に見立てられている。「不如帰の落し文」という言葉は、このような丸めた手紙を落とすのはホトトギスのしわざであるという考えに由来する。

Otoshi-bumi means dropped letter and refers to rolled-up leaves in which an insect (Apoderus jekelii) has laid its eggs. The fallen rolled-up leaves were likened to letters dropped on the roadside by which people conveyed secret messages to their lovers, etc. The phrase "*hototogisu no otoshi-bumi*" came from the idea that the lesser cuckoo dropped these rolled-up messages.

【雲の峰】
Kumo no mine

夏の盛りに見られる、青い空に高く聳え立つ山の峰のような形の雲のこと。大きく渦巻く雲は夏の特徴的な風景である。こうした雲は、強い日差しを受けて発生する激しい上昇気流が、温かく湿った空気を大気中に高く持ち上げることによって、いとも簡単にあらし雲へ成長していく。

Kumo no mine means cloud peak, that is, cloud formations which form during the height of summer and look like towering mountain peaks against the blue sky. Summer is characterized by large billowy clouds that easily develop into storm clouds due to the strong sunlight which creates powerful updrafts that lift the warm moist air high into the atmosphere.

【荒磯】
Araiso

荒い波が激しく打ちつける海岸線のこと。波の動きがとても強いので、海岸は浸食され、階段状の地形となる。この形状の海岸は魚類や貝類、海藻が豊富である。『万葉集』では、「あらいそ」と読まず「ありそ」と読まれている。

Araiso means the shoreline where rough waves break violently on the beach. The action of the waves is so strong that the coast is worn away and forms stair-like terraces. This type of shoreline is abundant in fish, shellfish, and *kaiso* "sea grasses." In the *Man'yoshu*, the word was pronounced "*ariso*," rather than "*araiso*."

〔鵜飼〕 *Ukai*

代表的な夏のイメージとなっている、鵜を使った漁法のこと。舟首でたくかがり火で鮎を引き寄せ、訓練した鵜に獲らせる。鵜は鮎を捕らえ、漁夫に向けて放す。5月の中旬から10月の中旬まで行われる。岐阜県の長良川、愛知県の木曽川、京都府の宇治川が鵜飼で有名。「鵜川」や「鵜籠」、「鵜篝」「鵜飼舟」など、鵜飼に関連する言葉は多い。

Ukai means cormorant fishing, which is a representative summer image. Trained cormorants are used to catch *ayu* "sweet fish," which are drawn to lanterns hanging from the prows of boats. The cormorants catch the *ayu* and release them for the fishermen. The fishing occurs from the middle of May to the middle of October. The Nagara River in Gifu Prefecture, the Kiso River in Aichi Prefecture, and the Uji River in Kyoto Prefecture are famous for their *ukai*. There are many words related to this activity, such as *ukawa* "cormorant river," *ukago* "cormorant basket (for holding the birds)," *ukagari* "the lanterns for fishing" and *ukaibune* "cormorant fishing boat."

【祭囃子】

Matsuri-bayashi

神社の祭りで演奏される音楽のこと。囃子方は笛や
数種類の太鼓、鉦をならし、行列の中の神輿に従っ
たり、山車の上に乗ったりもする。元々は、神を地上
に迎えるための音楽だった。江戸時代に、この音楽
がより洗練され、祭りに興奮と娯楽性を加えた。祇
園囃子（日本三大祭りのひとつである祇園祭のための音楽）
は、全国の祭囃子の発展に大きな
影響を与えた。

Matsuri-bayashi means music
played at shrine festivals. The
festival musicians usually play
flutes, several types of drums,
and gongs, and accompany the
mikoshi "sacred palanquin"
in processions, or ride on the
festival floats. Originally, the
hayashi was music used to wel-
come the *kami* "gods" when they came down to earth.
During the Edo Period (1603 – 1867), the music became
more refined and added excitement and entertainment
to the festival. The *Gion-bayashi* "music for the *Gion*
Festival (one of the three major festivals of Japan)" had
a great influence on the development of the *matsuri-
bayashi* of the entire country.

〔夕顔〕
Yugao

晩夏
―――
late

夕方に咲き、夜明けにしぼむ白い花のこと。平安貴族が観賞用の植物として育てはじめ、『源氏物語』の夕顔の巻の影響で歌に詠まれるようになった。この花は、植物と垣根のまわりを覆う巻きひげをもつ、つる植物である。食用瓢箪が実る唯一の植物でもある。

Yugao is a white flower that blooms in the evening and withers at dawn. It was grown as a decorative plant by the aristocracy of the Heian Period (794 – 1185) and appears in poetry from the influence of the "*Yugao*" chapter in *The Tale of Genji*. It grows from a vine which has curly tendrils that wrap around plants and fencing. The plant is also the only one which produces edible gourds.

〔舟遊び〕
Funa-asobi

夕方、涼をとるために海や湖、大きな川に舟を出すこと。屋根のついた大きな舟（屋形舟）、平底舟、簡単にシートの日覆いを掛けただけの船などがある。東京の隅田川の舟遊びは浮世絵によく描かれたが、滋賀の琵琶湖、長野の諏訪湖も舟遊びに人気の場所だった。

Funa-asobi means pleasure boating. To enjoy the coolness of the evening, people launched pleasure boats on the ocean, lakes, or large rivers. There were large roofed boats (*yakatabune*), barges, or smaller boats with simple cloth roofs. The Sumida River in Tokyo was well-known and often depicted in *ukiyoe* prints, but Lake Biwa in Shiga, and Lake Suwa in Nagano were also popular sites.

〔白雨〕

Haku-u

文字通りには白い雨のこと。午後遅くから、夕暮れ時にかけての突然の大雨をさす。雷を伴うことも多いが、少しすれば止み、空はたちまち晴れ上がる。雨のせいで景色が白色に見えるため白雨と呼ぶ。より一般的に使われる「夕立」の、より詩的な言葉である。

Haku-u literally means white rain. It refers to sudden, heavy rain falling from the late afternoon until dusk. It is often accompanied by thunder, but only lasts for a short while. Often the sky will clear up just as suddenly. It is called *haku-u* because the scenery appears white due to the rain. *Haku-u* is a more poetic word for the commonly-used word "*yudachi.*"

〔蝉時雨〕

Semishigure

晩夏
──○──
late

夏の間、蝉は木の幹にくっついて甲高い鳴き声を発する。蝉がいっせいに鳴き出すと、その鳴き声の大きさが時雨のように聞こえる。一方、ヒグラシの鳴き声には涼感がある。

Semishigure literally means cicada rainstorm. During the summer, cicadas clinging to the trunks of trees release a high-pitched buzzing sound in the heat. When the cicada begin to sing all at once, the loudness of their singing is compared to the sound of a sudden rainstorm. The song of the *higurashi* "evening cicada," on the other hand, has a cool feeling.

〔玉火〕

Tamabi

晚夏
———○———
late

文字通りには宝石の火という意味で、花火をさす。16世紀中頃に火薬や銃が日本に持ち込まれ、江戸時代にこの技術から生み出された花火が人気を博した。人々は、夜空を照らす花火の美しさ、そしてあっという間に消えてしまう花火のはかなさに魅了されてきた。「玉火」は初秋の季語だが、現在茶の湯では夏に用いられることが多い銘のため、晩夏のことばとして挙げた。

Tamabi literally means jewel fire and refers to fireworks. During the middle of the 16th century, gun powder and rifles were brought to Japan, and during the Edo Period (1603 – 1867), this technology was used to make fireworks, which became very popular. People have been fascinated by the beauty of fireworks lighting up the night sky and the fragile transiency of the fireworks which disappear in an instant. Although *tamabi* is a seasonal word for early autumn, it has been included in late summer because it is often use then in chanoyu.

季 節 に つ い て

日本人が季節をどのように考え、感じているかを理解するためには、
中国で季節を表すために用いられていた二十四節気というシステム
を知ることが大切です。このシステムはグレゴリオ暦とは異なります
が、理解するために重要なのは、二至二分（夏至と冬至、春分と秋分）
の中間点から季節が始まるということです。例えば、春は春分の日
である 3 月 21 日もしくは 22 日ではなく、約 1 ヶ月半前の 2 月 4 日も
しくは 5 日にはじまります。

したがって、各季節のはじまりは以下のようになります。

　　　2 月 4 日…立春、春のはじまり
　　　5 月 6 日…立夏、夏のはじまり
　　　8 月 8 日…立秋、秋のはじまり
　　　11 月 8 日…立冬、冬のはじまり

二至二分は各季節の分割点とみなされ、下記のように季節の中間と
されます。

　　　3 月 21 日…春分、春の中間日
　　　6 月 22 日…夏至、夏の中間日
　　　9 月 23 日…秋分、秋の中間日
　　　12 月 22 日…冬至、冬の中間日

各季節はさらに 6 つずつに分けられており、約 15 日ずつある各期
間の初日には中国の気候に由来する詩的な名前がつけられています。
二十四節気すべてのリストについては付録を参照してください。

The Seasons

In order to understand how Japanese think and feel about the seasons, it is important to understand the Chinese method of reckoning the seasons using a system called *Nijushi Sekki* "the 24 Point Seasonal Days." Although the system is different from the Gregorian calendar, the main point to understand is that in this system, the seasons are calculated to begin at the midpoint between the solstices and equinoxes. For example, spring begins around the 4th or 5th of February, rather than at the spring equinox on the 21st or 22nd of March, which is almost a month and a half earlier.

Thus, the beginnings of the seasons are, approximately, as follows:

> February 4th — *risshun*, beginning of spring
> May 6th — *rikka*, beginning of summer
> August 8th — *risshu*, beginning of autumn
> November 8th — *ritto*, beginning of winter

The equinoxes and solstices are considered to be the midpoint of the season, as seen here:

> March 21st — *shunbun*, middle day of spring
> June 22nd — *geshi*, middle day of summer
> September 23rd — *shubun*, middle day of autumn
> December 22nd — *toji*, middle day of winter

Each season is divided into six 15-day periods; the first day of each period is given a poetic name derived from the climate in China. See the appendix for a list of all of the 24 Point Seasonal Days.

二十四節気の暦は現代日本で公式には使用されていませんが、このような季節のはじまりのとらえ方は、未だに茶の湯で意識されています。例えば、風炉はふつう5月から10月まで使われますが、これは夏と秋にあたります。炉は11月から4月まで使われ、冬と春にあたります。

茶の湯の世界では、実際に自然界で起こっていることよりも先んじることが良いとされます。例えば、実際の春の盛りは4月で、二十四節気でいうと夏のはじまりに近い頃ですが、春がテーマのものは2月頃から使われはじめます。8月頃は夏の盛りで秋を感じるのは難しい季節ですが、この頃から秋の花が描かれた着物や道具が使われます。

いずれにせよ、二十四節気は日本の伝統文化、特に茶の湯、詩歌、芸術の世界に強い影響を与え続けています。現在もテレビの全国放送で二十四節気が知られ、現代の暦、特に茶の湯愛好家のためにつくられたものにはそれぞれの節気が記されています。季節の変化を味わうことは、日本の伝統文化の顕著な特徴であり、茶の湯を学ぶことは季節に対する感覚を持続させ、発展させることにつながっているのです。

Although the 24 Point Seasonal Days system is not officially used in modern Japan, this reckoning of the start of the seasons is still important for the world of chanoyu. For example, the *furo* "brazier" is used from May until October that corresponds with summer and autumn. The *ro* "open hearth" is used from November until April that corresponds with winter and spring.

There is a convention in the tea world to anticipate or be ahead of what is happening in the natural world. For example, spring themes and references will begin to be used around February, although the height of spring in April is closer to the beginning of summer in the 24 Point Seasonal Days system. Also, the designs of autumn flowers on kimono and utensils begin to appear around August, although it is the peak of the hot season, when there is hardly a feeling of autumn at all.

Whatever the case, the 24 Point Seasonal Days system continues to exert influence on the traditional culture of Japan, particularly the worlds of chanoyu, poetry, and art. Even today the 24 Point Seasonal Days are announced on national television, and modern calendars—especially those made for chanoyu enthusiasts—will include a notation of each of these days. The appreciation of the changing of the seasons is a salient feature of Japanese traditional culture, and the study of chanoyu encourages and promotes the continuity and development of seasonal awareness.

AUTUMN

8月 ― 10月
Aug. – Oct.

一年で最も暑い8月、暦の上では秋が訪れます。じりじりと暑い日々は続くも、徐々に陽の光には陰りが見え、時折吹く涼風に秋の気配を感じはじめます。やがて紅葉が色づき、虫の音が響く頃、風炉の名残を惜しむ季節がやってきます。

August is the hottest month of the year, but by the calendar, it is autumn. Scorching days continue, but gradually, the sun's rays weaken, and we can feel a hint of autumn in the cool, sporadic breezes. Eventually, around the time when the maples turn color, and the songs of the insects resound, the period of wistfulness about the last days of the brazier comes around again.

【精霊流し】 *Shoryonagashi*

初秋
○――
early

精霊流しとは、故人の魂が彼岸に戻る道を照らすために川や海に燈籠や供え物を浮かべること。盂蘭盆会（お盆とも）の３日間、先祖の魂はそれぞれの家へ迎えられる。最終日、人々はかがり火や燈籠などの送り火を灯す。地域の慣習に従って、ろうそくが置かれた小さな木片や、ろうそくを灯した箱型の浮かぶ燈籠、果物や野菜といった様々な供え物をつんだわら舟などが流される。

Shoryonagashi means to float lanterns or offerings on rivers or the ocean to light the way for the spirits of the deceased to return to the spirit world. The spirits are welcomed back to their ancestral homes during the three-day-long *Urabon'e* observance (often called *Obon*). On the last day, people light *okuribi* "send-off fires" which take the form of bonfires or *toro* "lanterns." Depending upon the local custom, small pieces of wood on which candles were placed, box-shaped floating lanterns lit by candles, or boats made of woven straw, which were filled with various offerings such as fruits and vegetables, were cast into the current.

〔白露〕

Hakuro

初秋
○
early

二十四節気のうちの一つで、秋分の15日前、9月8日頃にある。気温の低下にともなって露が降り、大気中の水蒸気が水滴となってでてくる。秋の夕方は寒いため木の葉や草に露が降りやすく、その様子は秋を代表する光景である。吹きさらしの葉から滴り落ち、光のもとで蒸発する露は、人間の存在とこの世の儚さを象徴しているが、これは「露の世」、「露の命」という言葉に表現されている。

Hakuro means white dew, and is the name of the one of the *Nijushi Sekki* days, occurring 15 days before *shubun* "the autumnal equinox" around September 8th. Dew forms as the temperature falls, and water droplets condense from the vapor in the air. Because the autumn evenings are cold, dew forms easily on the leaves of trees and grasses, and the image represents the feeling of autumn. Dew falls from the windblown leaves and evaporates in the sunlight symbolizing the transiency of this world and of human existence. This is expressed in the phrases *tsuyu no yo* "dew-like existence" and *tsuyu no inochi* "life as evanescent as the dew."

秋

八月―十月

【野分】
Nowaki

仲秋
—○—
mid

文字通りには野を分けるという意味で、野の草に吹きつけ、分かれさせる台風による強い風のこと。かつては木々を吹き倒し、野の草を平坦にする風の性質を知らず、嵐が過ぎ去った後の荒れ野にはある種の哀愁が感じられた。木々の葉が散らばり、萩や女郎花の上に折れた枝々が横たわるといった光景である。派生語に、「野分波」「野分雲」「野分晴」などがある。

Nowaki literally means dividing the fields and refers to the strong typhoon winds that flatten and part the grasses of the meadows. In the past people did not have knowledge about the nature of the winds which blew down trees and left tracks on the fields, and they felt a certain pathos in the roughened grasslands after the strong winds had passed. Leaves were scattered about and broken branches were lying over autumn flowers like *hagi* "bush clover" and *ominaeshi* "patrina." Phrases derived from this are *nowakinami* "waves of divided fields," *nowaki-gumo* "clouds driven by the strong winds" and *nowaki-bare* "clear weather after a typhoon."

【夜長】
Yonaga

長い夜のこと。一年で一番長い夜は12月の冬至だが、夜が長くなってきていると強く感じるのは9月や10月である。日の長い夏が過ぎ、日が短くなって残暑が落ち着くと、人々は読書や夜なべ仕事に打ち込む。

Yonaga means long night. Although the longest night of the year is the winter solstice in December, it is in September and October that we keenly feel the nights getting longer. After the long days of summer, the days become shorter; the lingering heat subsides; and people devote themselves to reading and night chores.

〔望月〕 *Mochizuki*

仲秋
—○—
mid

満月のこと。十五夜（陰暦の8月15日）に昇る仲秋の名月は、秋の最も美しい事象とされてきた。里芋、団子、枝豆、そして飾り用のすすきの房が供物台にのせられるが、これはもともと農耕的な儀式であったことを表わしている。里芋が旬を迎えるため、望月は「芋名月」とも呼ばれる。月見は、紅葉狩りや花見とあわせ、古くから人気である。

Mochizuki means the full moon. *Chushu no meigetsu* "the beautiful autumn moon" rises on *jugoya* "the 15th of the eighth lunar month." Taro potatoes, *dango* "pounded rice balls," edamame, and the tassels of *susuki* "miscanthus" were offered on an altar, indicating the original agricultural nature of the observance. *Mochizuki* is also called *imomeigetsu* because the *imo* "taro potatoes" were in season. Moon viewing, along with maple viewing and flower viewing, was a popular activity from ancient times.

〔十六夜〕

Jurokuya
(Izayoi)

仲秋
—○—
mid

陰暦 8 月 16 日の夜のこと。前夜の十五夜と比べると、十六夜の月はためらうように、少し遅れて昇る。「いざよい」とも呼ばれる。万葉時代には既に十六夜の月についての和歌が登場している。

Jurokuya literally means the night of the 16th day of the eighth lunar month. The moon rising on the 16th seems to hesitate and falter, rising a little later than *jugoya*, the previous night. It is also called *Izayoi* "hesitating moon." Poems about the moon of the 16th began to be written before the Man'yo Period (ca. 8th century).

〔初紅葉〕

Hatsumomiji

仲秋
—○—
mid

その年はじめての紅葉のこと。山頂や標高の高い場所で、山桜やハゼ、ナナカマドの葉が先駆けて赤く色づき、秋の到来を知らせる。秋の見せ場であるカエデの美しさがピークを迎えるのは、かなり後のことである。

Hatsumomiji means the first red leaves of the year. On the mountain peaks and at higher elevations, the leaves of the *yamazakura* "mountain cherry," *haze* "wax tree," and *nanakamado* "Japanese rowan" turn red earlier than other varieties and announce the coming of autumn. The maples, the highlight of autumn, reach their peak of beauty much later.

〔有明〕

Ariake

仲秋
—◦—
mid

夜明けのこと。早朝の薄暗い光の中に残っている月のことを「有明の月」という。秋分に最も近い満月の日の後、月の出はどんどん遅くなっていき、早朝にも残るようになる。早朝のかすかに輝く月はしばしば歌や絵の題材となった。関連する語に、「明けの月」「残る月」がある。

Ariake means the dawn, and the lingering moon in the dim light of early morning is called *ariake no tsuki*. After the moon appears at its peak closest to the autumnal equinox (*meigetsu*), it rises later and later and lingers into the early morning. The image of the faintly shining moon in the early morning was a favorite of poets and painters. Other phrases related to this were *ake no tsuki* "moon at daybreak" and *nokoru tsuki* "lingering moon."

〔鹿の声〕

Shika no koe

夕方に雄の鹿が求愛する声は悲しく哀れで、古人には秋の哀愁をあらわしているように聞こえた。鹿の鳴き声は古くから歌に詠まれ、平安時代には秋を代表する主題となった。詩や芸術作品の中では、鹿と一緒に紅葉が描かれることが多い。

Shika no koe means the call of the deer. The mating call of the male deer in the evening had a sad and pathetic sound, which seemed to embody the pathos of autumn to people in the olden days. Poems were written about the cry of the deer from before the Heian Period (794 – 1185), when it became a representative autumnal theme. Very often deer were depicted with maples in poetry and in art.

【着せ綿】

Kisewata

晩秋
○
late

香りと夜のうちに降りた露を吸うために、菊の上に置かれる綿のこと。9月9日の夜、菊の上に綿を置き、翌朝湿った綿で顔や体を拭いて、健康や長寿を祈願した。周の穆王（ぼくおう）に寵愛され、敵の策略のために山へ追放された菊慈童（きくじどう）の伝説に由来する。菊慈童は菊の露を飲み、不老不死となった。「菊寿」もこの伝説からきている。

Kisewata means cotton placed on the *kiku* "chrysanthemum plants" to absorb the fragrance and to capture the dew which forms at night. On the ninth night of the ninth month, cotton was placed on the chrysanthemum flowers and on the following morning, the dampened cotton was used to wipe the face and body as a prayer for good health and longevity. This custom derives from the legend of Kikujido "chrysanthemum child" who was favored by King Mu of the Zhou Dynasty (1046-256 BCE) and was banished to the mountains due to the plotting of his enemies. He drank the dew on the chrysanthemums and became immortal. *Kikuju* "chrysanthemum longevity" is derived from this legend.

【初雁】

Hatsukari

晩秋
———○
late

晩秋にやって来る、その年はじめての雁のこと。雁は頭部が長くずんぐりしており、体は灰色で尾が短い。古来、雁の悲しげな鳴き声は非常に賞賛され、特に秋の空を一列になって飛んでくる初雁の声が良いとされた。雁が登場する歌は『万葉集』にもみられ、それ以前には既に秋を連想させる詩の主題となっていた。

Hatsukari refers to the first geese that arrive in late autumn of the year. The geese have long heads on fat, gray bodies and short tails. From ancient times, the plaintive cries of the geese were much admired, particularly when they first began to arrive, flying in straight lines against the autumn sky. Poems about geese appeared in the *Man'yoshu*, and by that time they had already become a seasonal poetic theme for autumn.

【落穂】

Ochibo

晩秋
———○
late

穀物の落穂、一般的には落ちた稲穂のこと。稲が刈り取られた後、穂が田や稲架の下、畦沿いに落ちる。農家の人々が一粒も無駄にしないよう落穂を集めていくことを、「落穂拾い」といった。

Ochibo means fallen ears of grain, generally rice. After the rice stalks were cut, ears of grain fell on the fields, along the paths, and under the drying racks. In order not to waste even a single grain, farmers gathered the fallen ears, an activity called *ochibo hiroi* "picking up the fallen rice ears."

〔虫の音〕

Mushi no ne

虫の鳴き声のこと。コオロギやキリギリスといった虫の鳴き声をまとめてさした句。こうした虫は一般的に夕方や夜に鳴き、秋の夜の寂しさをいっそう強くさせる。鳴き声を楽しむため、コオロギや鈴虫、松虫を「虫籠」と呼ばれる籠に入れて育てた。

Mushi no ne means the chirping of insects. This phrase refers collectively to the songs of a varieties of crickets and Japanese katydids. These insects generally chirp in the evening and night, and intensify the desolate feeling of the autumn. *Korogi* "cricket," *suzumushi* "bell cricket," and *matsumushi* "pine cricket" were raised in baskets called *mushikago* so that people could enjoy their chirping more easily.

〔龍田姫〕
Tatsuta-hime

かつての都、平城京の西に位置する龍田山の化身。西は秋の方角とされて、春をつかさどる佐保姫に対し、龍田姫は秋をつかさどる。龍田山の紅葉の美しさを詠んだ歌は、万葉時代からあった。

Tatsuta-hime means Princess Tatsuta, who is a personification of Mt. Tatsuta, a mountain to the west of the ancient capital Heijokyo. The west is considered to be the direction of autumn, and Tatsuta-hime rules over the autumn, in contrast to Sao-hime, the princess who rules over spring. Poems about the beauty of the autumn foliage at Mt. Tatsuta were written from the Man'yo Period (ca. 8th century).

〔手向山〕
Tamukeyama

晩秋
——。
late

奈良の東大寺の東側にある、紅葉の名所の山のこと。菅原道真の有名な歌で取り上げられており、「このたびは幣も取りあへず手向山　紅葉の錦神のまにまに」（宇多天皇の御幸の安全を祈って道ばたの神の石像にお供えしたいが、適当なお供えを用意して来られなかったので、かわりに紅葉を捧げます）と詠まれている。

Tamukeyama is a mountain famous for its autumn colors, located to the east of the Todaiji temple in Nara. It is featured in a well-known poem by Sugawara Michizane in which he writes that he would have liked to present proper offerings to the statue of the traveller's guardian deity to pray for the safe travel of Emperor Uda (867-931). These were not prepared beforehand, so instead, he would like to offer the colored autumn foliage of Tamukeyama.

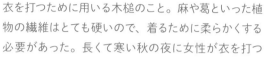

秋

八月—十月

〔砧〕
Kinuta

衣を打つために用いる木槌のこと。麻や葛といった植物の繊維はとても硬いので、着るために柔らかくする必要があった。長くて寒い秋の夜に女性が衣を打つ音には哀愁がある。中国や日本で、遠くから聞こえる砧を打つ音が詠まれた。

Kinuta means a wooden fulling mallet used for beating cloth. The fibers of hemp, kudzu, and other plants were very stiff and needed to be softened for clothing. The sound of women pounding the cloth during the long, cold autumn nights conveyed a very desolate-feeling. In China and Japan, poems were written about the sound of the *kinuta* in the distance.

〔夕霧〕
Yugiri

夕方にかかる霧のこと。空気が地上の冷気に近づくと、水蒸気が水滴となって地上に浮かび、煙に覆われているように見える。同じ現象は春にも起こるが、これは霧というより霞と呼ばれる。水滴が大きくなると細かい雨のように降るが、これは「霧雨」「霧時雨」と呼ばれる。

Yugiri means evening mist. As the air close to the ground cools, water vapor turns to droplets which float about the ground giving the appearance that it is covered with smoke. This same phenomenon happens in spring, but it is called *ka-sumi*, rather than *kiri*. When the droplets become larger, they fall like a fine rain called *kirisame*, or *kirishigure*.

88

〔山里〕
Yamazato

山深くに集まる質素な農家を想起させる語。素朴な生活を求めて都会の喧騒から離れ、田舎の優雅な生活をひとりで送ることを理想とする考え方が中国から渡来した。茶人たちはやがて簡素な茶室を建てることで「市中の山居」という理想を体現した。
しちゅう　さんきょ

Yamazato means mountain village and conjures the image of rustic farm houses clustered in the deep mountains. From China came the ideal of removing one's self from the bustling city in search of a simple, elegant life in rustic surroundings. Japanese tea masters built simple *chashitsu* "tea huts or tea rooms" to embody the ideal of *shichu no sankyo* "mountain hermitage in the city."

〔唐錦〕
Karanishiki

晩秋
—○—
late

文字通りには、中国から渡来した錦のことで、鮮やかで豪華な織物のような、山腹の美しい紅葉のことをさす。この光景を表わす他の語に「山の錦」「野山の錦」「秋の錦」がある。

Karanishiki means imported Chinese brocade and refers to the beauty of the leaves on the mountainsides that appear like colorful, richly woven fabric. Other words using this imagery are *yama no nishiki* "mountain brocade," *noyama no nishiki* "field and mountain brocade" and *aki no nishiki* "autumn brocade."

茶 の 湯 の 主 客

茶室では、亭主と客が取り合わせと呼ばれる道具組を通して心を通わせます。亭主はおもてなしの心をあらわす方法として、道具を取り合わせてテーマを表現します。亭主の努力や思いに応えるため、客の代表である正客は関心と感謝の心をもって茶席にのぞみ、使われている全ての道具を拝見します。ふつう、取り合わせは1年のうち決まった時期のために選ばれるので、それぞれの茶席で異なる道具が取り合わせられます。一例をあげると、一年の中の代表的な茶席に初茶会があります。このめでたい機会に、亭主はお祝いの意味やおめでたい意味をもつ道具を取り合わせます。

裏千家家元の初釜式では、新年のはじまりを祝うために伝統的な道具と新たに作られた道具が使われます。毎年床の間に荘られる多くの道具のほかに、お家元は「七草」という銘がついた瀬戸茶入を使われます。新年7日目に、健康のために七草で味つけをしたおかゆをたべる習慣があるからです。この名前には新鮮さ、そして新年にふさわしい春めいた感じがあります。

お家元は、「みやこ」「あづま」「なにわ」という銘をもつ、三碗がセットになった樂茶碗も使います。この銘は日本の伝統文化の中心である三つの都のことで、さらに言えば日本全国、また新年を祝い平和と繁栄を願うために集まった茶人を象徴しています。

Guest and Host in the Tearoom

In the tea room, the host and guest build a rapport and connection through the assemblage of utensils for the gathering, which is called *toriawase*. The host coordinated the utensils to refer to or to express a certain concept or idea as a means of showing his hospitality to his guests. In order to respond to the host's efforts and feelings, the main guest, who has the role of representative of the guests, engages the host by showing his interest in and appreciation of all of the utensils being used. Generally, the *toriawase* will be specially selected for a certain time of the year, and each tea gathering will have a different *toriawase*. As an example, one of the most representative tea gatherings on the yearly calendar is the *hatsuchakai* "first tea gathering of the year." For this happy occasion, the host will assemble objects which have celebratory or auspicious meanings.

At the *Hatsugama no Shiki* "the First Tea Gathering Ceremony of the Year" Sen Soshitsu XVI, the grand tea master of the *Urasenke* Tradition of the Way of Tea, uses heirloom utensils and newly-ordered objects to celebrate the beginning of the New Year. In addition to the objects in the alcove, which are used every year, the grand master uses a Seto ware *chaire* "thick tea container" with the poetic name *Nanakusa* "The Seven Grasses of Spring." The *gomei* refers to the custom of eating rice gruel flavored with the *nanakusa* for good health on the 7th day of the new year. This name has a fresh and spring-like quality that is considered appropriate for New Year's.

The grand tea master uses a stacked set of three *Raku*-ware tea bowls, which have the names, *Miyako* "Kyoto," *Azuma* "Tokyo," and *Naniwa* "Osaka." These *gomei* refer to the three capitals that are centers of traditional culture, and that, by extension, represent the entire nation and the *chajin* who are joined together through chanoyu to celebrate New Year's and to pray for peace and prosperity.

初釜に用いられる薄茶器は羽衣棗と呼ばれるもので、天女が天に帰るために必要な羽衣を返してもらうために舞を舞う能の演目からきています。この棗は、この演目の舞台であり富士山の美しい景色で有名な三保の松原の松の枝からつくられています。胴回りに松皮が残っており、羽衣の意匠の豪華な蒔絵がほどこされています。

また富士山は、日本で最も高い山として、また神聖な場所として、しばしば新年のお祝いの図像や取り合わせに用いられます。富士山の高く、荘厳で、完璧な形に、めでたいお祝いの意味が重ね合わせられます。

初釜式には、家元が茶杓を削り、それにふさわしい銘を付ける習慣もあります。その銘はおめでたい雰囲気のあるものだったり、その年の干支に関係があるものだったりします。歴史的価値や正月らしさ、歴代の家元との縁などの理由から毎年使用される道具も多いですが、銘や文様、由来、特定の関係といった理由から、新しい道具や特別な道具が取り合わせに加えられます。

亭主のもてなしに対して関心があること示すために、正客は全ての道具について上手に尋ね、道具に関する情報や作家、由来、取り合わせ全体における意味、茶道具同士の関連などを共有するため、亭主と客は茶会の間会話を続けます。客が亭主の意図に汲みとることができればできるほど、茶席は楽しいものとなります。この心のこもったコミュニケーションを通して、亭主と客は一座建立、つまり仲間意識と参加者の結束感をつくりあげるのです。

The thin tea container for *Hatsugama no shiki* is called *Hagoromo*, referring to the noh play *Hagoromo* in which a *tennyo* "celestial being" performs a dance in order to reclaim her robe of feathers that will enable her to return to heaven. The *natsume* "thin tea container" itself is made from a pine branch from Miho no Matsubara, a pine grove renowned for its view of Mt. Fuji and the setting for the play. The *natsume*, which retains the pine bark around the body, is decorated with a gorgeous, gold-lacquered design of the robe of feathers.

Mt. Fuji, as the tallest mountain in Japan and a sacred place, often appears in *toriawase* for celebratory New Year's gatherings. Its height, majesty, and perfect shape have many overlapping auspicious and celebratory meanings.

It is the custom for the grand tea master to carve a *chashaku* "bamboo tea scoop" and to give it an appropriate *gomei* that has a celebratory feeling, or, perhaps, refers to the *eto* "Chinese zodiac animal" for that year. Although many of the utensils are used every year because of their historic value, appropriateness for the New Year, or their relationship to one of the past grand tea masters, new or special objects are also incorporated into the *toriawase* because of their *gomei*, their design, their provenance, or specific references.

To show his appreciation for the host's hospitality, the main guest skillfully asks questions about all of the utensils, and he and host carry on a running dialogue during the gathering to share information about the utensils, their makers and provenance, their meaning in the overall scheme, and the references and relationship between the objects. The more that the guests can respond to the host's intentions, the more enjoyable tea gathering becomes. Through this heartfelt communication, the host and the guests create *Ichiza konryu*, the feeling of camaraderie and bonding among all the participants.

WINTER

———————————

11月 — 12月
Nov. – Dec.

茶人の正月とも称される炉開きとともに、冬の
取り合わせが幕を開けます。だんだんと景色
が色を失い、寒さが身に沁みていく季節になぞ
らえた銘の数々。湯気をたてる一服のお茶を
味わいながら、行く年を振り返ります。

With the opening of the hearth, which is called the
tea person's New Year's, the curtain rises on winter
toriawase "assemblage of tea utensils." Slowly
the colors in the scenery disappear, and there are
many *gomei* which delineate the season when the
cold penetrates the body. As we enjoy a bowl of
tea from which steam rises, we look back at the
departing year.

〔木守〕

Kimamori

初冬
○———
early

文字通り言うと、木を守る人のこと。冬になると、果実がたっぷりと実って、重く頭をたれた秋の柿の木の枝が遠い夢のように感じられる。葉が落ちると、柿の実がひとつだけ高い枝に残されているのをよく見かける。来年の豊作を祈って、冬の間実をひとつ残しておくのである。小鳥のために残しているともいわれる。

Kimamori literally means protector of the tree. The memory of the drooping branches of the persimmon tree heavily laden with fruit during the autumn seems like a distant dream. After all of the leaves have fallen, a single persimmon remaining on a high branch is often seen. One fruit is left on the tree during the winter to pray for an abundant harvest the next year. It is also said that the fruit is left for the little birds.

〔木枯らし〕

Kogarashi

初冬
○———
early

冬の到来を告げる、強い北風のこと。木枯らしは晩秋か初冬に吹く。10月下旬から11月上旬、強い風が木々の葉を吹き散らし、景色が冬めく。関連語の「冬の風」は、冬の活気がなく空虚なイメージをさした言葉。

Kogarashi refers to the strong northern wind that announces the coming of winter. *Kogarashi* occurs in either late autumn or early winter. In late October or early November, strong winds blow the leaves from the trees, and the scenery takes on a wintery aspect. *Fuyu no kaze* "winter wind" is a related phrase, and its overall image has a lifeless, empty quality.

〔玄猪〕 *Gencho*

初冬
○——
early

陰暦 10 月の亥の日の祝いのこと。子孫繁栄を祈ってこの日に餅を食べる中国の慣習に基づいている。猪はたくさんの子供を産むため、多産の象徴である。日本で、この餅は「亥の子餅」「玄猪餅」と呼ばれる。

Gencho means celebration of the wild boar day, held on the first day of the boar in the 10th lunar month. It is based on a Chinese custom of eating *mochi* "pounded sticky rice" on this day to pray for perpetuation of a family's descendants. The boar gives birth to many offspring and is a symbol of fertility. In Japan, this *mochi* is called *inoko mochi* "boarlet rice sweet" or *gencho mochi*.

〔時雨〕

Shigure

初冬
○——
early

初冬に思いがけず降るにわか雨のこと。天気が非常に変わりやすく、短い期間で降ったり止んだりを繰り返す。京都の詩歌にしばしば時雨が詠まれていることからも、時雨が京都周辺でよく見られていたことがわかる。この雨によってだんだんと活気がなくなり、冬の寂しさが増し、自然界の色が徐々に消えていく。先人達は、儚さの中にある美しさを大切にした。関連語に「村時雨」、「北山時雨」、「時雨雲」がある。

Shigure means sudden rain showers occurring in early winter. The weather is extremely changeable, and it rains and clears in rapid succession. *Shigure* was very common in the Kyoto environs as indicated by the large number of poems, written by Kyoto poets in the past that mention the phenomena. The sudden showers slowly drain the color of the natural world—the liveliness of the scenery slowly declines, becoming desolate and forlorn. People in the olden days developed an appreciation of beauty found in transiency. Related words are *murashigure* "sudden rain in the country village," *kitayamashigure* "sudden shower from the northern mountains of Kyoto" and *shigure-gumo* "sudden shower clouds."

〔初霜〕

Hatsushimo

初冬
○——
early

その年はじめて降りる霜のこと。寒く冴えた夜の翌早朝に霜が降りやすく、冬の訪れを感じさせる。色づいた落葉の上や湿った田畑、荒れた野原に氷の結晶の薄い層がみられる。日が昇ると空気があたたかくなり、霜はたちまち溶ける。

Hatsushimo means the first frost which forms in the winter of that year. Frost will often form in the early morning after a cold, clear evening, and the arrival of winter can be felt. At dawn a thin layer of ice crystals is seen on the fallen, colored leaves, on the damp earth of the rice paddies, and on the deserted fields. After the sun comes out and warms the air, the frost melts away very quickly.

〔冬木立〕

Fuyukodachi

葉が全て落ち、むきだしの枝を空に向かって伸ばしながら林立する、はかない木々のこと。「夏木立」の豊かな緑葉と対照的に、ものさびしさが感じられる。似た語に「枯れ木立」、「冬木」、「寒林」などがある。

Fuyukodachi means barren trees in the winter. It refers to a grove of deciduous trees that have dropped all of their leaves, so that their bare branches stand out starkly against the sky. The lonely feeling of the image contrasts with that of *natsukodachi* "a stand of trees with luxuriant green leaves in the summer." Related words are *kare-kodachi* "withered stand of trees," *fuyuki* "winter tree(s)," and *kanrin* "cold grove."

【冬籠り】

Fuyu-gomori

冬の間、屋内に籠もっていること。また、動物の冬眠や植物の休眠の期間のこと。

Fuyu-gomori means to stay indoors during the winter. It also indicates hibernation or a rest period for the plants and animals.

【年忘れ】

Toshiwasure

仲冬
―○―
mid

過ぎ行く年の辛苦を忘れ、新年の健康と安全を祈るために、友達、家族、同僚と集まること。年忘れという言葉は室町時代にはじめて登場し、年の終わりに先祖を祀る行事だった。その習慣が絶えて、現在は宗教的な意味合いはなく、年末の集まりは「忘年会」と呼ばれる。

Toshiwasure means forget the year and refers to gatherings with friends, family, and colleagues to dispel memories of the hardships of the past year and to pray for good health and protection against disaster in the New Year. The term *toshiwasure* first appears in the Muromachi Period (1336 – 1573), when it was the custom to honor the ancestors at the end of the year. This custom has died out, and now *toshiwasure* has no religious connotations. End of the year gatherings are now called *bonenkai* "forgetting the year party."

〔札納め〕 　　　*Fuda-osame*　　　仲冬
　　　　　　　　　　　　　　　　　　　—o—
　　　　　　　　　　　　　　　　　　　mid

年末に古いお札を寺社へ納めること。また、寺社に集まった
お札を焼く行事のこと。お札は火事や災害、病気、悪運か
ら家を守るために家に貼られる。新年には新しいお札を求め
るため、古いお札を納めることは新年を迎える準備のひとつ。

Fuda-osame means to take *ofuda* "old wooden or paper
talismans" to temples or shrines at the end of the year.
Also, it refers to the ceremony in which the talismans
that have been brought to the shrine or temple are rit-
ually burned. The *ofuda* are put up in homes to protect
the household against fire, disasters, disease, and bad
fortune. Disposing of the old *ofuda* is done as part of
the preparations for New Year's when new ones will be
purchased.

〔年の瀬〕

Toshi no se

仲冬
——∘——
mid

年末のこと。12月の中頃から、年の終わりが迫って
くるように感じられる。かつては、12月13日（江戸で
は12月8日）は「事始め」といい、新年の準備がはじ
まる日だった。今日では忘年会を開いたり、お歳暮を
贈ったり、年賀状を書いたりと、皆が忙しく過ごす。

Toshi no se means the end of the year. It is the period beginning
from the middle of December when the end of the year seems
to be pressing in. In olden times, *kotohajime* on the 13th day of
the 12th month (8th day of the 12th month in Edo) was the day on
which preparations for New Year's began. Nowadays everyone is
busy with year-end parties, sending *oseibo* "end of the year pres-
ents," and writing *nengajo* "New Year's cards."

〔枯野〕

Kareno

晩冬
——∘——
late

冬枯れの野原のこと。単に枯れた野原や田畑、森
だけではなく、冬の農村や様々な田園風景をも想起
させる言葉。中世以後、枯野は詩歌によく登場する。
枯野という言葉から連想される荒れ果てた状態の中に、
「わび」に通じる美が見出された。関連語に「冬野」、
「冬の原」がある。

Kareno means dried fields in the winter. The image includes not
just dried fields of grasses, rice paddies, forests, but also farming
villages and various rural scenes in the winter. From the medieval
period onward, *kareno* was a popular image that often appeared
in poetry. It suggested a desolate beauty related to the idea of
wabi (quiet, rustic beauty found in chanoyu). Related words are
fuyuno "winter field(s)" and *fuyu no hara* "winter moor."

〔埋み火〕

Uzumibi

炉の中で、火のついた炭を灰で覆い、火種を朝まで消さないようにする習慣。翌朝、埋み火は炉や火鉢の火をつけるための火種とする。茶の湯では、大晦日の除夜釜に使用した炭を灰に埋めておき、元日の夜明け前、埋めた火を使って大福茶と呼ばれる新年最初の茶を点てる。

Uzumibi means buried fire and refers to the custom of covering lit charcoal with ash in the *ro* "sunken hearth" to keep it smoldering overnight. The next morning, the buried charcoal is used as a starter flame to light the hearth and *hibachi* "heating braziers." In chanoyu, the charcoal from *Joyagama* "New Year's Eve tea gathering" is buried in the ash. Before dawn on New Year's Day, the charcoal is taken out to light the fire for the first tea called *Obukucha* "Great Prosperity Tea."

〔柴の雪〕

Shiba no yuki

柴の上に積もった雪のこと。小枝を集めて束にし、燃料にした。小枝の上に積もった雪はわびを感じさせる。小枝を縦に束ねて作る柴垣と言う囲いもある。

晩冬
—○—
late

Shiba no yuki means snow on the brushwood. Small branches from trees were gathered into bundles to be used for kindling. The snow accumulating on the twigs conveyed a very *wabi* feeling. There is also a kind of fencing (*shibagaki*) made by lashing together vertical bundles of twigs.

〔浦千鳥〕

Urachidori

海辺にいる千鳥のこと。千鳥は、かつて渡り鳥と留鳥両方を含む、海の近くに住む小さな鳥の総称だった。近頃は短いくちばしと灰色の羽根をもつ鳥に限定して使われる。千鳥は非常に人気の画題で、波や水の模様と合わせて描かれる。関連する語に「磯千鳥」、「村千鳥」「友千鳥」などがある。

Urachidori are *chidori* "plovers" by the seashore. In the past, *chidori* was a general word for small birds, both migratory and non-migratory types that lived near the ocean. Nowadays, it refers specifically to the plovers, which have short beaks and gray feathers. *Chidori* are a popular art motif often paired with waves and water designs. (*Chidori* is a winter *gomei*, although it is often used during the summer). Related words are *isochidori* "seashore plovers," *murachidori* "flocking plovers" and *tomochidori* "flock of plovers."

〔風花〕　　*Kazahana*

晩冬
——○
late

冴えわたった冷たい空に舞い落ちる雪片のこと。雪
になるかと思っているうちに、いつのまにか消えて
しまう。冬の詩歌に好んで詠まれる言葉。「かざはな」はこの美し
い情景にぴったりの発音だが、「かざばな」ともいう。

Kazahana means wind flower and refers to snowflakes which
flutter down in a clear, cold sky. As we wonder if it will continue to snow, the flakes disappear. It is one of the favorite
words of poets when writing about the winter and may be
pronounced *kazahana* or *kazabana*, although the former pronunciation is said to have a more appropriate sound for this
beautiful occurrence.

〔寒月〕

Kangetsu

晩冬
——○
late

他の季節の月と比べると、冬の寒さのせいもあり、冴
えた空にのぼる冬の月はさびしげで、冷え冷えとして
いるように感じられる。冬の風が雪を吹き払い、澄ん
だ空に輝く月の光は見る者の心を動かす。関連する
語に、「冬の月」、「月氷る」がある。

Kangetsu means cold moon. Compared to the moons of the
other three seasons, the colorless moon rising in the clear winter sky takes on a lonely, desolate, and chilling feeling because
of the psychological effect of the cold. The intense moonlight
in the sky, swept clear of snow by the winter wind, moves the
hearts of people who gaze upon it. Related words are *fuyu no
tsuki* "winter moon," and *tsuki koru* "the moon freezes."

付録

四季と二十四節気

For Seasons & 24 Point Seasonal Days

 春　SPRING

2月4日頃 around Feb. 4	りっしゅん 立 春 *Risshun*	春の気が立つ。一年の始まり。 Beginning of spring
2月19日頃 around Feb. 19	う　すい 雨 水 *Usui*	氷雪が解け、雪が雨に変わる。 Rain water
3月6日頃 around Mar. 6	けい ちつ 啓 蟄 *Keichitsu*	冬眠していた虫が穴から這い出す。 Awakening of insects
3月21日頃 around Mar. 21	しゅん ぶん 春 分 *Shunbun*	太陽黄経が0度で、昼夜同じ長さ。 Vernal equinox, middle of spring
4月5日頃 around Apr. 5	せい めい 清 明 *Seimei*	天地が清浄で、草木の芽が出る。 Clear and bright (skies)
4月20日頃 around Apr. 20	こく　う 穀 雨 *Koku-u*	雨が降り、穀物が生育する。 Grain rain

夏　SUMMER

5月6日頃 around May 6	りっか 立 夏 *Rikka*	夏の気が立つ。 Beginning of summer
5月21日頃 around May 21	しょうまん 小 満 *Shoman*	陽気さかんで万物が満ちる。 Grain full
6月6日頃 around June 6	ぼうしゅ 芒 種 *Boshu*	芒のある穀物の種をまく。 Grain in ear
6月22日頃 around June 22	げし 夏 至 *Geshi*	太陽黄経が90度で、昼が最長の日。 Summer solstice, middle of summer
7月8日頃 around July 8	しょうしょ 小 暑 *Shosho*	本格的な暑さが始まる。 Little heat
7月23日頃 around July 23	たいしょ 大 暑 *Taisho*	暑さが最高になる。 Great heat

秋　AUTUMN

8月8日頃 around Aug. 8	りっしゅう 立 秋 *Risshu*	秋の気が立つ。 Beginning of autumn
8月24日頃 around Aug. 24	しょ しょ 処 暑 *Shosho*	暑さがおさまる。 End of heat
9月8日頃 around Sept. 8	はく ろ 白 露 *Hakuro*	大気が冷えて露が降り始める。 White dew
9月23日頃 around Sept. 23	しゅう ぶん 秋 分 *Shubun*	太陽黄経が180度で、昼夜同じ長さ。 Autumnal equinox, middle of autumn
10月9日頃 around Oct. 9	かん ろ 寒 露 *Kanro*	草花に冷たい露が宿る。 Cold dew
10月24日頃 around Oct. 24	そう こう 霜 降 *Soko*	霜が降りて草木が枯れ始める。 Descent of frost

WINTER

11月8日頃 around Nov. 8	りっ とう 立 冬 *Ritto*	冬の気が立つ。 Beginning of winter
11月23日頃 around Nov. 23	しょう せつ 小 雪 *Shosetsu*	雨が雪になり始める。 Little snow
12月8日頃 around Dec. 8	たい せつ 大 雪 *Taisetsu*	雪が積もり始める。 Great snow
12月22日頃 around Dec. 22	とう じ 冬 至 *Toji*	太陽黄経が270度で、夜が最長の日。 Winter solstice, middle of winter
1月6日頃 around Jan. 6	しょう かん 小 寒 *Shokan*	寒さがきびしくなる。 Little cold
1月20日頃 around Jan. 20	たい かん 大 寒 *Daikan*	寒さが最高になる。 Great cold

索引

著者略歴

ブルース・濱名 宗整（ぶるーす はまな そうせい）

1951年、米国・ハワイ州生まれ。ハワイ大学卒業後、裏千家学園茶道専門学校外国人研修コースおよび茶道科で裏千家茶道を学ぶ。1986年、今日庵外事部に入庵し、英字季刊誌『裏千家ニューズレター』の編集や海外行事の企画・運営に携わるなど、裏千家茶道の海外普及に尽力。現在は同専門学校外国人研修コース講師、裏千家国際セミナー講師などを務める。監修書に『イラストで覚える！茶の湯英単語』（淡交社）がある。

イラスト　　木村明美
デザイン　　瀧澤弘樹

英語で伝える茶の湯の銘100
100 Beautiful Words in the Way of Tea

2020年7月15日　　初版発行

著　者　　ブルース・濱名宗整
発行者　　納屋嘉人
発行所　　株式会社 淡交社
　　　　　本社　〒603-8588　京都市北区堀川通鞍馬口上ル
　　　　　営業　075-432-5151　編集　075-432-5161
　　　　　支社　〒162-0061　東京都新宿区市谷柳町39-1
　　　　　営業　03-5269-7941　編集　03-5269-1691
　　　　　www.tankosha.co.jp
印刷・製本　株式会社ムーブ

©2020 ブルース・濱名宗整　Printed in Japan
ISBN978-4-473-04400-6